This Journal Belongs To

If Found, Please Return

Phone:

Email:

Questions For Life:

Two Year Guided Daily Journal For Intentional Living

Jessica A. Walsh

A comparative guided daily journal for recording two years of events, gratitude, happiness, and reflections worthy of remembrance.

HOW TO USE THIS BOOK

You can begin using this journal at any point in the year. Turn to today's calendar date and fill in the year at the top of that page's first entry. Record some thoughts or events regarding the present day, list what you're grateful for on this particular day, what your happiest moment was, and answer the question asked. Do the same every day for a year. When you return to where you started, record your responses for year two in the lower blank entry space. Reflect on your previous year's responses as you fill the remainder of the journal.

Cover design by Shelley Shayner (www.shelleyshayner.com)

JANUARY 1, 20____

About Today: _____

_____

_____

_____

You're Grateful For: _____

Your Happiest Moment Was: _____

_____

_____

What Do You Want To Achieve This Year?_____

_____

_____

JANUARY 1, 20____

About Today: _____

_____

_____

_____

You're Grateful For:_____

Your Happiest Moment Was: _____

_____

_____

What Do You Want To Achieve This Year?_____

_____

_____

JANUARY 2, 20____

About Today: _____

_____

_____

_____

You're Grateful For: _____

Your Happiest Moment Was: _____

_____

_____

Did You Make Good Use Of Your Time Today? _____

_____

_____

JANUARY 2, 20____

About Today: _____

_____

_____

_____

You're Grateful For: _____

Your Happiest Moment Was: _____

_____

_____

Did You Make Good Use Of Your Time Today? _____

_____

_____

JANUARY 3, 20____

About Today: _____

_____

_____

_____

You're Grateful For: _____

Your Happiest Moment Was: _____

_____

_____

Where Do You Find Inspiration? _____

_____

_____

JANUARY 3, 20____

About Today: _____

_____

_____

_____

You're Grateful For: _____

Your Happiest Moment Was: _____

_____

_____

Where Do You Find Inspiration? _____

_____

_____

JANUARY 4, 20____

About Today: _____

_____

_____

_____

You're Grateful For: _____

Your Happiest Moment Was: _____

_____

_____

Do You Own Your Belongings Or Do They Own You? _____

_____

_____

JANUARY 4, 20____

About Today: _____

_____

_____

_____

You're Grateful For: _____

Your Happiest Moment Was: _____

_____

_____

Do You Own Your Belongings Or Do They Own You? _____

_____

_____

JANUARY 5, 20____

About Today: _____

_____

_____

_____

You're Grateful For: _____

Your Happiest Moment Was: _____

_____

_____

Do The People You Love Most Know How Much You Love Them? _____

_____

_____

JANUARY 5, 20____

About Today: _____

_____

_____

_____

You're Grateful For: _____

Your Happiest Moment Was: _____

_____

_____

Do The People You Love Most Know How Much You Love Them? _____

_____

_____

JANUARY 6, 20____

About Today: _____

_____

_____

_____

You're Grateful For: _____

Your Happiest Moment Was: _____

_____

_____

What's Your Favorite Holiday & Why? _____

_____

_____

JANUARY 6, 20____

About Today: _____

_____

_____

_____

You're Grateful For: _____

Your Happiest Moment Was: _____

_____

_____

What's Your Favorite Holiday & Why? _____

_____

_____

JANUARY 7, 20____

About Today: _____

_____

_____

_____

You're Grateful For: _____

Your Happiest Moment Was: _____

_____

_____

In What Ways Are You The Same As Your Childhood-Self? _____

_____

_____

JANUARY 7, 20____

About Today: _____

_____

_____

_____

You're Grateful For: _____

Your Happiest Moment Was: _____

_____

_____

In What Ways Are You The Same As Your Childhood-Self? _____

_____

_____

JANUARY 8, 20____

About Today: _____

_____

_____

_____

You're Grateful For: _____

Your Happiest Moment Was: _____

_____

_____

What Makes You Feel Accomplished? _____

_____

_____

JANUARY 8, 20____

About Today: _____

_____

_____

_____

You're Grateful For: _____

Your Happiest Moment Was: _____

_____

_____

What Makes You Feel Accomplished? _____

_____

_____

JANUARY 9, 20___

About Today: _____

_____

_____

_____

You're Grateful For:_____

Your Happiest Moment Was: _____

_____

_____

What Bad Habits Do You Want To Break? _____

_____

_____

JANUARY 9, 20___

About Today: _____

_____

_____

_____

You're Grateful For:_____

Your Happiest Moment Was: _____

_____

_____

What Bad Habits Do You Want To Break? _____

_____

_____

JANUARY 10, 20____

About Today: _____

_____

_____

_____

You're Grateful For: _____

Your Happiest Moment Was: _____

_____

_____

What Brings You Down Most Often? _____

_____

_____

JANUARY 10, 20____

About Today: _____

_____

_____

_____

You're Grateful For: _____

Your Happiest Moment Was: _____

_____

_____

What Brings You Down Most Often? _____

_____

_____

JANUARY 11, 20____

About Today: _____

_____

_____

_____

You're Grateful For: _____

Your Happiest Moment Was: _____

_____

_____

What Do You Want For Your Birthday? _____

_____

_____

JANUARY 11, 20____

About Today: _____

_____

_____

_____

You're Grateful For: _____

Your Happiest Moment Was: _____

_____

_____

What Do You Want For Your Birthday? _____

_____

_____

JANUARY 12, 20____

About Today: _____

_____

_____

_____

You're Grateful For:_____

Your Happiest Moment Was: _____

_____

_____

What's Your Idea Of A Perfect Weekend? _____

_____

_____

JANUARY 12, 20____

About Today: _____

_____

_____

_____

You're Grateful For:_____

Your Happiest Moment Was: _____

_____

_____

What's Your Idea Of A Perfect Weekend? _____

_____

_____

JANUARY 13, 20____

About Today: _____

_____

_____

_____

You're Grateful For: _____

Your Happiest Moment Was: _____

_____

_____

How Would You Describe Yourself? _____

_____

_____

JANUARY 13, 20____

About Today: _____

_____

_____

_____

You're Grateful For: _____

Your Happiest Moment Was: _____

_____

_____

How Would You Describe Yourself? _____

_____

_____

JANUARY 14, 20____

About Today: _____

_____

_____

_____

You're Grateful For:_____

Your Happiest Moment Was: _____

_____

_____

Was Today Lucky Or Unlucky? Why? _____

_____

_____

JANUARY 14, 20____

About Today: _____

_____

_____

_____

You're Grateful For:_____

Your Happiest Moment Was: _____

_____

_____

Was Today Lucky Or Unlucky? Why? _____

_____

_____

JANUARY 15, 20___

About Today: _____

_____

_____

_____

You're Grateful For: _____

Your Happiest Moment Was: _____

_____

_____

What Lesson Did You Learn The Hard Way? _____

_____

_____

JANUARY 15, 20___

About Today: _____

_____

_____

_____

You're Grateful For: _____

Your Happiest Moment Was: _____

_____

_____

What Lesson Did You Learn The Hard Way? _____

_____

_____

JANUARY 16, 20____

About Today: _____

_____

_____

_____

You're Grateful For: _____

Your Happiest Moment Was: _____

_____

_____

How Do You Define Family? _____

_____

_____

JANUARY 16, 20____

About Today: _____

_____

_____

_____

You're Grateful For: _____

Your Happiest Moment Was: _____

_____

_____

How Do You Define Family? _____

_____

_____

JANUARY 17, 20____

About Today: _____

_____

_____

_____

You're Grateful For: _____

Your Happiest Moment Was: _____

_____

_____

What's The Bravest Thing You've Ever Done? _____

_____

_____

JANUARY 17, 20____

About Today: _____

_____

_____

_____

You're Grateful For: _____

Your Happiest Moment Was: _____

_____

_____

What's The Bravest Thing You've Ever Done? _____

_____

_____

JANUARY 18, 20____

About Today: _____

_____

_____

_____

You're Grateful For: _____

Your Happiest Moment Was: _____

_____

_____

Do You Consider Yourself To Be Creative? Why Or Why Not? _____

_____

_____

JANUARY 18, 20____

About Today: _____

_____

_____

_____

You're Grateful For: _____

Your Happiest Moment Was: _____

_____

_____

Do You Consider Yourself To Be Creative? Why Or Why Not? _____

_____

_____

JANUARY 19, 20____

About Today: _____

_____

_____

_____

You're Grateful For: _____

Your Happiest Moment Was: _____

_____

_____

Does What You're Currently Wearing Make You Feel Good About Yourself?

_____

_____

JANUARY 19, 20____

About Today: _____

_____

_____

_____

You're Grateful For: _____

Your Happiest Moment Was: _____

_____

_____

Does What You're Currently Wearing Make You Feel Good About Yourself?

_____

_____

JANUARY 20, 20____

About Today: _____

_____

_____

_____

You're Grateful For:_____

Your Happiest Moment Was: _____

_____

_____

What Was The Last Thing You Did That Made You Feel Proud?_____

_____

_____

JANUARY 20, 20____

About Today: _____

_____

_____

_____

You're Grateful For:_____

Your Happiest Moment Was: _____

_____

_____

What Was The Last Thing You Did That Made You Feel Proud?_____

_____

_____

JANUARY 21, 20____

About Today: _____

_____

_____

_____

You're Grateful For: _____

Your Happiest Moment Was: _____

_____

_____

In What Ways Do You Hold Yourself Back? _____

_____

_____

JANUARY 21, 20____

About Today: _____

_____

_____

_____

You're Grateful For: _____

Your Happiest Moment Was: _____

_____

_____

In What Ways Do You Hold Yourself Back? _____

_____

_____

JANUARY 22, 20____

About Today: _____

_____

_____

_____

You're Grateful For:_____

Your Happiest Moment Was: _____

_____

_____

If You Could Time Travel, Would You Visit The Past Or Future? _____

_____

_____

JANUARY 22, 20____

About Today: _____

_____

_____

_____

You're Grateful For:_____

Your Happiest Moment Was: _____

_____

_____

If You Could Time Travel, Would You Visit The Past Or Future? _____

_____

_____

JANUARY 23, 20____

About Today: _____

_____

_____

_____

You're Grateful For: _____

Your Happiest Moment Was: _____

_____

_____

Do You Really Listen When People Talk To You? _____

_____

_____

JANUARY 23, 20____

About Today: _____

_____

_____

_____

You're Grateful For: _____

Your Happiest Moment Was: _____

_____

_____

Do You Really Listen When People Talk To You? _____

_____

_____

JANUARY 24, 20____

About Today: _____

_____

_____

_____

You're Grateful For:_____

Your Happiest Moment Was: _____

_____

_____

What Was The #1 Item On Your To-Do List Today? Did You Complete It?

_____

_____

JANUARY 24, 20____

About Today: _____

_____

_____

_____

You're Grateful For:_____

Your Happiest Moment Was: _____

_____

_____

What Was The #1 Item On Your To-Do List Today? Did You Complete It?

_____

_____

JANUARY 25, 20___

About Today: _____

_____

_____

_____

You're Grateful For:_____

Your Happiest Moment Was: _____

_____

_____

Which Parent Are You Closest To & Why?_____

_____

JANUARY 25, 20___

About Today: _____

_____

_____

_____

You're Grateful For:_____

Your Happiest Moment Was: _____

_____

_____

Which Parent Are You Closest To & Why?_____

_____

JANUARY 26, 20____

About Today: _____

_____

_____

_____

You're Grateful For:_____

Your Happiest Moment Was: _____

_____

_____

Is There Anyone In Your Life You'd Like To Forgive, But Haven't? _____

_____

_____

JANUARY 26, 20____

About Today: _____

_____

_____

_____

You're Grateful For:_____

Your Happiest Moment Was: _____

_____

_____

Is There Anyone In Your Life You'd Like To Forgive, But Haven't? _____

_____

_____

JANUARY 27, 20____

About Today: _____

_____

_____

_____

You're Grateful For: _____

Your Happiest Moment Was: _____

_____

_____

What Makes You Feel Alive? _____

_____

_____

JANUARY 27, 20____

About Today: _____

_____

_____

_____

You're Grateful For: _____

Your Happiest Moment Was: _____

_____

_____

What Makes You Feel Alive? _____

_____

_____

JANUARY 28, 20____

About Today: _____
_____
_____
_____

You're Grateful For: _____

Your Happiest Moment Was: _____
_____
_____

Which Is Worse: Failing Or Never Trying? _____
_____
_____

JANUARY 28, 20____

About Today: _____
_____
_____
_____

You're Grateful For: _____

Your Happiest Moment Was: _____
_____
_____

Which Is Worse: Failing Or Never Trying? _____
_____
_____

JANUARY 29, 20____

About Today: _____

_____

_____

_____

You're Grateful For: _____

Your Happiest Moment Was: _____

_____

_____

What's One Of Your Sexual Fantasies?_____

_____

_____

JANUARY 29, 20____

About Today: _____

_____

_____

_____

You're Grateful For: _____

Your Happiest Moment Was: _____

_____

_____

What's One Of Your Sexual Fantasies?_____

_____

_____

JANUARY 30, 20____

About Today: _____

_____

_____

_____

You're Grateful For:_____

Your Happiest Moment Was:_____

_____

_____

What's Your Favorite Movie & Why Does It Speak To You?_____

_____

_____

JANUARY 30, 20____

About Today: _____

_____

_____

_____

You're Grateful For:_____

Your Happiest Moment Was:_____

_____

_____

What's Your Favorite Movie & Why Does It Speak To You?_____

_____

_____

JANUARY 31, 20____

About Today: _____

_____

_____

_____

You're Grateful For:_____

Your Happiest Moment Was: _____

_____

_____

What Do You Want To Accomplish By The End Of February?_____

_____

_____

JANUARY 31, 20____

About Today: _____

_____

_____

_____

You're Grateful For:_____

Your Happiest Moment Was: _____

_____

_____

What Do You Want To Accomplish By The End Of February?_____

_____

_____

Don't wait for everything to be perfect before you decide to enjoy your life.

-Joyce Meyer

FEBRUARY 1, 20___

About Today: _____

_____

_____

_____

You're Grateful For: _____

Your Happiest Moment Was: _____

_____

_____

Do You Say *Yes* When You Really Want To Say *No*? Why? _____

_____

_____

FEBRUARY 1, 20___

About Today: _____

_____

_____

_____

You're Grateful For: _____

Your Happiest Moment Was: _____

_____

_____

Do You Say *Yes* When You Really Want To Say *No*? Why? _____

_____

_____

FEBRUARY 2, 20____

About Today: _____

_____

_____

_____

You're Grateful For:_____

Your Happiest Moment Was: _____

_____

_____

What Hobby Are You Interested In, But Haven't Tried Yet?_____

_____

_____

FEBRUARY 2, 20____

About Today: _____

_____

_____

_____

You're Grateful For:_____

Your Happiest Moment Was: _____

_____

_____

What Hobby Are You Interested In, But Haven't Tried Yet?_____

_____

_____

FEBRUARY 3, 20____

About Today: _____

_____

_____

_____

You're Grateful For:_____

Your Happiest Moment Was: _____

_____

_____

Do You Own Uncomfortable Shoes? If So, Why Do You Keep Them? _____

_____

_____

FEBRUARY 3, 20____

About Today: _____

_____

_____

_____

You're Grateful For:_____

Your Happiest Moment Was: _____

_____

_____

Do You Own Uncomfortable Shoes? If So, Why Do You Keep Them? _____

_____

_____

FEBRUARY 4, 20___

About Today: _____
_____
_____
_____

You're Grateful For:_____

Your Happiest Moment Was: _____
_____
_____

Do The People In Your Life Bring Out The Best In You? _____
_____
_____

FEBRUARY 4, 20___

About Today: _____
_____
_____
_____

You're Grateful For:_____

Your Happiest Moment Was: _____
_____
_____

Do The People In Your Life Bring Out The Best In You? _____
_____
_____

FEBRUARY 5, 20____

About Today: _____

_____

_____

_____

You're Grateful For: _____

Your Happiest Moment Was: _____

_____

_____

What Makes You Cry? _____

_____

_____

FEBRUARY 5, 20____

About Today: _____

_____

_____

_____

You're Grateful For: _____

Your Happiest Moment Was: _____

_____

_____

What Makes You Cry? _____

_____

_____

FEBRUARY 6, 20____

About Today: _____

_____

_____

_____

You're Grateful For: _____

Your Happiest Moment Was: _____

_____

_____

What Did You Learn Today? _____

_____

_____

FEBRUARY 6, 20____

About Today: _____

_____

_____

_____

You're Grateful For: _____

Your Happiest Moment Was: _____

_____

_____

What Did You Learn Today? _____

_____

_____

FEBRUARY 7, 20____

About Today: _____

_____

_____

_____

You're Grateful For: _____

Your Happiest Moment Was: _____

_____

_____

Do You Like Who You Are? _____

_____

_____

FEBRUARY 7, 20____

About Today: _____

_____

_____

_____

You're Grateful For: _____

Your Happiest Moment Was: _____

_____

_____

Do You Like Who You Are? _____

_____

_____

FEBRUARY 8, 20___

About Today: _____

_____

_____

_____

You're Grateful For:_____

Your Happiest Moment Was: _____

_____

_____

If You Could Live One Day Over & Over Again, How Would You Spend It?

_____

_____

FEBRUARY 8, 20___

About Today: _____

_____

_____

_____

You're Grateful For:_____

Your Happiest Moment Was: _____

_____

_____

If You Could Live One Day Over & Over Again, How Would You Spend It?

_____

_____

FEBRUARY 9, 20____

About Today: _____
_____
_____
_____

You're Grateful For: _____

Your Happiest Moment Was: _____
_____
_____

What's Your Greatest Strength? _____
_____
_____

FEBRUARY 9, 20____

About Today: _____
_____
_____
_____

You're Grateful For: _____

Your Happiest Moment Was: _____
_____
_____

What's Your Greatest Strength? _____
_____
_____

FEBRUARY 10, 20____

About Today: _____
_____
_____
_____

You're Grateful For:_____

Your Happiest Moment Was:_____
_____
_____

What Are Some Of Your Pet Peeves?_____
_____
_____

FEBRUARY 10, 20____

About Today: _____
_____
_____
_____

You're Grateful For:_____

Your Happiest Moment Was:_____
_____
_____

What Are Some Of Your Pet Peeves?_____
_____
_____

FEBRUARY 11, 20____

About Today: _____

_____

_____

_____

You're Grateful For: _____

Your Happiest Moment Was: _____

_____

_____

When Is The Last Time You Rode A Bicycle? _____

_____

_____

FEBRUARY 11, 20____

About Today: _____

_____

_____

_____

You're Grateful For: _____

Your Happiest Moment Was: _____

_____

_____

When Is The Last Time You Rode A Bicycle? _____

_____

_____

FEBRUARY 12, 20____

About Today: _____

_____

_____

_____

You're Grateful For:_____

Your Happiest Moment Was: _____

_____

_____

If You Could Give Your Childhood-Self Advice, What Would It Be?

_____

_____

FEBRUARY 12, 20____

About Today: _____

_____

_____

_____

You're Grateful For:_____

Your Happiest Moment Was: _____

_____

_____

If You Could Give Your Childhood-Self Advice, What Would It Be?

_____

_____

FEBRUARY 13, 20____

About Today: _____

_____

_____

_____

You're Grateful For:_____

Your Happiest Moment Was: _____

_____

_____

Are You Enriching The Lives Of Others? Whose?_____

_____

_____

FEBRUARY 13, 20____

About Today: _____

_____

_____

_____

You're Grateful For:_____

Your Happiest Moment Was: _____

_____

_____

Are You Enriching The Lives Of Others? Whose?_____

_____

_____

FEBRUARY 14, 20____

About Today: _____

_____

_____

_____

You're Grateful For: _____

Your Happiest Moment Was: _____

_____

_____

How Do You Show Yourself Love? _____

_____

_____

FEBRUARY 14, 20____

About Today: _____

_____

_____

_____

You're Grateful For: _____

Your Happiest Moment Was: _____

_____

_____

How Do You Show Yourself Love? _____

_____

_____

FEBRUARY 15, 20____

About Today: _____

_____

_____

_____

You're Grateful For: _____

Your Happiest Moment Was: _____

_____

_____

Did You Exercise Today? If Not, Why? _____

_____

_____

FEBRUARY 15, 20____

About Today: _____

_____

_____

_____

You're Grateful For: _____

Your Happiest Moment Was: _____

_____

_____

Did You Exercise Today? If Not, Why? _____

_____

_____

FEBRUARY 16, 20____

About Today: _____

_____

_____

_____

You're Grateful For: _____

Your Happiest Moment Was: _____

_____

_____

What Does Success Mean To You? _____

_____

_____

FEBRUARY 16, 20____

About Today: _____

_____

_____

_____

You're Grateful For: _____

Your Happiest Moment Was: _____

_____

_____

What Does Success Mean To You? _____

_____

_____

FEBRUARY 17, 20____

About Today: _____

_____

_____

_____

You're Grateful For: _____

Your Happiest Moment Was: _____

_____

_____

How Does Your Living Space Reflect Your Inner World? _____

_____

_____

FEBRUARY 17, 20____

About Today: _____

_____

_____

_____

You're Grateful For: _____

Your Happiest Moment Was: _____

_____

_____

How Does Your Living Space Reflect Your Inner World? _____

_____

_____

FEBRUARY 18, 20____

About Today: _____
_____
_____
_____

You're Grateful For:_____

Your Happiest Moment Was:_____
_____
_____

Do You Own Anything That Makes You Feel Sad Or Angry When You See It?
_____
_____

FEBRUARY 18, 20____

About Today: _____
_____
_____
_____

You're Grateful For:_____

Your Happiest Moment Was:_____
_____
_____

Do You Own Anything That Makes You Feel Sad Or Angry When You See It?
_____
_____

FEBRUARY 19, 20___

About Today: _____

_____

_____

_____

You're Grateful For: _____

Your Happiest Moment Was: _____

_____

_____

Were Your Parents Too Strict Or Too Lenient? _____

_____

_____

FEBRUARY 19, 20___

About Today: _____

_____

_____

_____

You're Grateful For: _____

Your Happiest Moment Was: _____

_____

_____

Were Your Parents Too Strict Or Too Lenient? _____

_____

FEBRUARY 20, 20___

About Today: _____

_____

_____

_____

You're Grateful For:_____

Your Happiest Moment Was: _____

_____

_____

When Was The Last Time You Lied? Why? _____

_____

_____

FEBRUARY 20, 20___

About Today: _____

_____

_____

_____

You're Grateful For:_____

Your Happiest Moment Was: _____

_____

_____

When Was The Last Time You Lied? Why? _____

_____

_____

FEBRUARY 21, 20____

About Today: _____

_____

_____

_____

You're Grateful For: _____

Your Happiest Moment Was: _____

_____

_____

If You Could Be Invisible For One Day, What Would You Do? _____

_____

_____

FEBRUARY 21, 20____

About Today: _____

_____

_____

_____

You're Grateful For: _____

Your Happiest Moment Was: _____

_____

_____

If You Could Be Invisible For One Day, What Would You Do? _____

_____

_____

FEBRUARY 22, 20____

About Today: _____

_____

_____

_____

You're Grateful For:_____

Your Happiest Moment Was: _____

_____

_____

What's Your Biggest Dream? _____

_____

_____

FEBRUARY 22, 20____

About Today: _____

_____

_____

_____

You're Grateful For:_____

Your Happiest Moment Was: _____

_____

_____

What's Your Biggest Dream? _____

_____

_____

FEBRUARY 23, 20____

About Today: _____

_____

_____

_____

You're Grateful For: _____

Your Happiest Moment Was: _____

_____

_____

How Do You Like To Be Supported? _____

_____

_____

FEBRUARY 23, 20____

About Today: _____

_____

_____

_____

You're Grateful For: _____

Your Happiest Moment Was: _____

_____

_____

How Do You Like To Be Supported? _____

_____

_____

FEBRUARY 24, 20____

About Today: _____

_____

_____

_____

You're Grateful For:_____

Your Happiest Moment Was: _____

_____

_____

Were You Patient Or Impatient Today? _____

_____

_____

FEBRUARY 24, 20____

About Today: _____

_____

_____

_____

You're Grateful For:_____

Your Happiest Moment Was: _____

_____

_____

Were You Patient Or Impatient Today? _____

_____

_____

FEBRUARY 25, 20____

About Today: _____

_____

_____

_____

You're Grateful For: _____

Your Happiest Moment Was: _____

_____

_____

What Worries You Most About The Future? _____

_____

_____

FEBRUARY 25, 20____

About Today: _____

_____

_____

_____

You're Grateful For: _____

Your Happiest Moment Was: _____

_____

_____

What Worries You Most About The Future? _____

_____

_____

FEBRUARY 26, 20____

About Today: _____

_____

_____

_____

You're Grateful For: _____

Your Happiest Moment Was: _____

_____

_____

When Was The Last Time You Tried Something New? _____

_____

_____

FEBRUARY 26, 20____

About Today: _____

_____

_____

_____

You're Grateful For: _____

Your Happiest Moment Was: _____

_____

_____

When Was The Last Time You Tried Something New? _____

_____

_____

FEBRUARY 27, 20___

About Today: _____

_____

_____

_____

You're Grateful For: _____

Your Happiest Moment Was: _____

_____

_____

Another Month Has Gone. What Did You Accomplish? _____

_____

_____

FEBRUARY 27, 20___

About Today: _____

_____

_____

_____

You're Grateful For: _____

Your Happiest Moment Was: _____

_____

_____

Another Month Has Gone. What Did You Accomplish? _____

_____

_____

FEBRUARY 28, 20____

About Today: _____

_____

_____

_____

You're Grateful For: _____

Your Happiest Moment Was: _____

_____

_____

What Do You Want To Accomplish By The End Of March? _____

_____

_____

FEBRUARY 28, 20____

About Today: _____

_____

_____

_____

You're Grateful For: _____

Your Happiest Moment Was: _____

_____

_____

What Do You Want To Accomplish By The End Of March? _____

_____

_____

FEBRUARY 29, 20___ *(If Leap Year)*

About Today: _____

_____

_____

_____

You're Grateful For: _____

Your Happiest Moment Was: _____

_____

_____

Is Today A Leap Day? If So, How Did You Use The Extra Time? _____

_____

_____

FEBRUARY 29, 20___

About Today: _____

_____

_____

_____

You're Grateful For: _____

Your Happiest Moment Was: _____

_____

_____

Is Today A Leap Day? If So, How Did You Use The Extra Time? _____

_____

_____

Creativity is intelligence having fun.

-Albert Einstein

MARCH 1, 20___

About Today: _____

_____

_____

_____

You're Grateful For: _____

Your Happiest Moment Was: _____

_____

_____

If You Could Take A Plane Anywhere Right Now, Where Would You Go?

_____

_____

MARCH 1, 20___

About Today: _____

_____

_____

_____

You're Grateful For: _____

Your Happiest Moment Was: _____

_____

_____

If You Could Take A Plane Anywhere Right Now, Where Would You Go?

_____

_____

MARCH 2, 20___

About Today: _____

_____

_____

_____

You're Grateful For:_____

Your Happiest Moment Was: _____

_____

_____

When Was The Last Time You Napped? How Did It Make You Feel?

_____

_____

MARCH 2, 20___

About Today: _____

_____

_____

_____

You're Grateful For:_____

Your Happiest Moment Was: _____

_____

_____

When Was The Last Time You Napped? How Did It Make You Feel?

_____

_____

MARCH 3, 20____

About Today: _____

_____

_____

_____

You're Grateful For:_____

Your Happiest Moment Was: _____

_____

_____

If You Could Master A Skill You Don't Currently Possess, What Would It Be?

_____

_____

MARCH 3, 20____

About Today: _____

_____

_____

_____

You're Grateful For:_____

Your Happiest Moment Was: _____

_____

_____

If You Could Master A Skill You Don't Currently Possess, What Would It Be?

_____

_____

MARCH 4, 20____

About Today: _____

_____

_____

_____

You're Grateful For:_____

Your Happiest Moment Was: _____

_____

_____

Would Getting Rid Of 50 Items In Your Home Be An Easy or Difficult Task?

_____

_____

MARCH 4, 20____

About Today: _____

_____

_____

_____

You're Grateful For:_____

Your Happiest Moment Was: _____

_____

_____

Would Getting Rid Of 50 Items In Your Home Be An Easy or Difficult Task?

_____

_____

MARCH 5, 20____

About Today: _____

_____

_____

_____

You're Grateful For: _____

Your Happiest Moment Was: _____

_____

_____

Are You Satisfied With The Amount Of Time You Spend With Your Family?

_____

_____

MARCH 5, 20____

About Today: _____

_____

_____

_____

You're Grateful For: _____

Your Happiest Moment Was: _____

_____

_____

Are You Satisfied With The Amount Of Time You Spend With Your Family?

_____

_____

MARCH 6, 20____

About Today: _____

_____

_____

_____

You're Grateful For: _____

Your Happiest Moment Was: _____

_____

_____

Have You Performed Any Acts Of Kindness Recently? _____

_____

_____

MARCH 6, 20____

About Today: _____

_____

_____

_____

You're Grateful For: _____

Your Happiest Moment Was: _____

_____

_____

Have You Performed Any Acts Of Kindness Recently? _____

_____

_____

MARCH 7, 20___

About Today: _____

_____

_____

_____

You're Grateful For: _____

Your Happiest Moment Was: _____

_____

_____

Do You Feel You Wasted Time Today? If So, Doing What? _____

_____

_____

MARCH 7, 20___

About Today: _____

_____

_____

_____

You're Grateful For: _____

Your Happiest Moment Was: _____

_____

_____

Do You Feel You Wasted Time Today? If So, Doing What? _____

_____

_____

MARCH 8, 20____

About Today: _____
_____
_____
_____

You're Grateful For: _____

Your Happiest Moment Was: _____
_____
_____

What Motivates You – External Or Internal Factors? _____
_____
_____

MARCH 8, 20____

About Today: _____
_____
_____
_____

You're Grateful For: _____

Your Happiest Moment Was: _____
_____

What Motivates You – External Or Internal Factors? _____
_____
_____

MARCH 9, 20____

About Today: _____

_____

_____

_____

You're Grateful For: _____

Your Happiest Moment Was: _____

_____

_____

Do You Think You're Worthy Of Love, Affection & Respect? _____

_____

_____

MARCH 9, 20____

About Today: _____

_____

_____

_____

You're Grateful For: _____

Your Happiest Moment Was: _____

_____

_____

Do You Think You're Worthy Of Love, Affection & Respect? _____

_____

_____

MARCH 10, 20___

About Today: _____

_____

_____

_____

You're Grateful For:_____

Your Happiest Moment Was: _____

_____

_____

What Valuable Lesson Could Someone Learn From Your Life? _____

_____

_____

MARCH 10, 20___

About Today: _____

_____

_____

_____

You're Grateful For:_____

Your Happiest Moment Was: _____

_____

_____

What Valuable Lesson Could Someone Learn From Your Life? _____

_____

_____

MARCH 11, 20____

About Today: _____

_____

_____

_____

You're Grateful For:_____

Your Happiest Moment Was: _____

_____

_____

How Often Do The Conversations In Your Head Go The Same Way In Reality?

_____

_____

MARCH 11, 20____

About Today: _____

_____

_____

_____

You're Grateful For:_____

Your Happiest Moment Was: _____

_____

_____

How Often Do The Conversations In Your Head Go The Same Way In Reality?

_____

_____

MARCH 12, 20____

About Today: _____

_____

_____

_____

You're Grateful For:_____

Your Happiest Moment Was: _____

_____

_____

If You Could Have An Exotic Animal For A Pet, Which Would You Choose?

_____

_____

MARCH 12, 20____

About Today: _____

_____

_____

_____

You're Grateful For:_____

Your Happiest Moment Was: _____

_____

_____

If You Could Have An Exotic Animal For A Pet, Which Would You Choose?

_____

_____

MARCH 13, 20____

About Today: _____

_____

_____

_____

You're Grateful For:_____

Your Happiest Moment Was: _____

_____

_____

Which Of Your Friends Are You Most Proud Of? Why? _____

_____

_____

MARCH 13, 20____

About Today: _____

_____

_____

_____

You're Grateful For:_____

Your Happiest Moment Was: _____

_____

_____

Which Of Your Friends Are You Most Proud Of? Why? _____

_____

_____

MARCH 14, 20___

About Today: _____

_____

_____

_____

You're Grateful For: _____

Your Happiest Moment Was: _____

_____

_____

What Are You Doing When You Feel Most Confident? _____

_____

_____

MARCH 14, 20___

About Today: _____

_____

_____

_____

You're Grateful For: _____

Your Happiest Moment Was: _____

_____

_____

What Are You Doing When You Feel Most Confident? _____

_____

_____

MARCH 15, 20____

About Today: _____

_____

_____

_____

You're Grateful For:_____

Your Happiest Moment Was: _____

_____

_____

Did You Hit The Snooze Button Today? How Many Times? _____

_____

_____

MARCH 15, 20____

About Today: _____

_____

_____

_____

You're Grateful For:_____

Your Happiest Moment Was: _____

_____

_____

Did You Hit The Snooze Button Today? How Many Times? _____

_____

_____

MARCH 16, 20____

About Today: _____

_____

_____

_____

You're Grateful For:_____

Your Happiest Moment Was: _____

_____

_____

What Are Things You'd Like To Change About Yourself? _____

_____

_____

MARCH 16, 20____

About Today: _____

_____

_____

_____

You're Grateful For:_____

Your Happiest Moment Was: _____

_____

_____

What Are Things You'd Like To Change About Yourself? _____

_____

_____

MARCH 17, 20____

About Today: _____

_____

_____

_____

You're Grateful For: _____

Your Happiest Moment Was: _____

_____

_____

What Time Of Day Do You Feel Most Creative? _____

_____

_____

MARCH 17, 20____

About Today: _____

_____

_____

_____

You're Grateful For: _____

Your Happiest Moment Was: _____

_____

_____

What Time Of Day Do You Feel Most Creative? _____

_____

_____

MARCH 18, 20____

About Today: _____
_____
_____
_____

You're Grateful For:_____

Your Happiest Moment Was:_____
_____
_____

What Are Your Thoughts On The Saying *Less Is More*?_____
_____
_____

MARCH 18, 20____

About Today: _____
_____
_____
_____

You're Grateful For:_____

Your Happiest Moment Was:_____
_____
_____

What Are Your Thoughts On The Saying *Less Is More*?_____
_____
_____

MARCH 19, 20____

About Today: _____

_____

_____

_____

You're Grateful For: _____

Your Happiest Moment Was: _____

_____

_____

What Do You Miss Most From Childhood? _____

_____

_____

MARCH 19, 20____

About Today: _____

_____

_____

_____

You're Grateful For: _____

Your Happiest Moment Was: _____

_____

_____

What Do You Miss Most From Childhood? _____

_____

_____

MARCH 20, 20____

About Today: _____

_____

_____

_____

You're Grateful For:_____

Your Happiest Moment Was: _____

_____

_____

If Your Life Were A Movie, Would You Enjoy Watching It? _____

_____

_____

MARCH 20, 20____

About Today: _____

_____

_____

_____

You're Grateful For:_____

Your Happiest Moment Was: _____

_____

_____

If Your Life Were A Movie, Would You Enjoy Watching It? _____

_____

MARCH 21, 20____

About Today: _____

_____

_____

_____

You're Grateful For: _____

Your Happiest Moment Was: _____

_____

_____

What Would You Want To Eat For Your Last Meal? _____

_____

_____

MARCH 21, 20____

About Today: _____

_____

_____

_____

You're Grateful For: _____

Your Happiest Moment Was: _____

_____

_____

What Would You Want To Eat For Your Last Meal? _____

_____

_____

MARCH 22, 20____

About Today: _____

_____

_____

_____

You're Grateful For:_____

Your Happiest Moment Was: _____

_____

_____

Where Are You Living Right Now: The Past, Present Or Future?

_____

_____

MARCH 22, 20____

About Today: _____

_____

_____

_____

You're Grateful For:_____

Your Happiest Moment Was: _____

_____

_____

Where Are You Living Right Now: The Past, Present Or Future?

_____

_____

MARCH 23, 20____

About Today: _____

_____

_____

_____

You're Grateful For: _____

Your Happiest Moment Was: _____

_____

_____

What Do You Love Most About Your Father? Does/Did He Know?

_____

_____

MARCH 23, 20____

About Today: _____

_____

_____

_____

You're Grateful For: _____

Your Happiest Moment Was: _____

_____

_____

What Do You Love Most About Your Father? Does/Did He Know?

_____

_____

MARCH 24, 20____

About Today: _____

_____

_____

_____

You're Grateful For:_____

Your Happiest Moment Was: _____

_____

_____

Where Do You Feel Safe? _____

_____

_____

MARCH 24, 20____

About Today: _____

_____

_____

_____

You're Grateful For:_____

Your Happiest Moment Was: _____

_____

_____

Where Do You Feel Safe? _____

_____

_____

MARCH 25, 20____

About Today: _____

_____

_____

_____

You're Grateful For: _____

Your Happiest Moment Was: _____

_____

_____

Are You Satisfied With Today? _____

_____

_____

MARCH 25, 20____

About Today: _____

_____

_____

_____

You're Grateful For: _____

Your Happiest Moment Was: _____

_____

_____

Are You Satisfied With Today? _____

_____

_____

MARCH 26, 20___

About Today: _____

_____

_____

_____

You're Grateful For: _____

Your Happiest Moment Was: _____

_____

_____

What Do You Wish You Knew Ten Years Ago? _____

_____

_____

MARCH 26, 20___

About Today: _____

_____

_____

_____

You're Grateful For: _____

Your Happiest Moment Was: _____

_____

_____

What Do You Wish You Knew Ten Years Ago? _____

_____

_____

MARCH 27, 20___

About Today: _____

_____

_____

_____

You're Grateful For: _____

Your Happiest Moment Was: _____

_____

_____

How Often Do You Let Your Fears Hold You Back? _____

_____

_____

MARCH 27, 20___

About Today: _____

_____

_____

_____

You're Grateful For: _____

Your Happiest Moment Was: _____

_____

How Often Do You Let Your Fears Hold You Back? _____

_____

_____

MARCH 28, 20____

About Today: _____

_____

_____

_____

You're Grateful For:_____

Your Happiest Moment Was: _____

_____

_____

How Do You Like To Relax & Unwind? _____

_____

_____

MARCH 28, 20____

About Today: _____

_____

_____

_____

You're Grateful For:_____

Your Happiest Moment Was: _____

_____

_____

How Do You Like To Relax & Unwind? _____

_____

_____

MARCH 29, 20____

About Today: _____

_____

_____

_____

You're Grateful For: _____

Your Happiest Moment Was: _____

_____

_____

What's The Most Beautiful Place You've Ever Been? _____

_____

_____

MARCH 29, 20____

About Today: _____

_____

_____

_____

You're Grateful For: _____

Your Happiest Moment Was: _____

_____

What's The Most Beautiful Place You've Ever Been? _____

_____

_____

MARCH 30, 20___

About Today: _____

_____

_____

_____

You're Grateful For:_____

Your Happiest Moment Was:_____

_____

_____

Another Month Has Gone. What Made You Feel Proud This Month?_____

_____

_____

MARCH 30, 20___

About Today: _____

_____

_____

_____

You're Grateful For:_____

Your Happiest Moment Was: _____

_____

_____

Another Month Has Gone. What Made You Feel Proud This Month?_____

_____

_____

MARCH 31, 20____

About Today: _____

_____

_____

_____

You're Grateful For: _____

Your Happiest Moment Was: _____

_____

_____

What Do You Want To Accomplish By The End Of April?____

_____

_____

MARCH 31, 20____

About Today: _____

_____

_____

_____

You're Grateful For: _____

Your Happiest Moment Was: _____

_____

_____

What Do You Want To Accomplish By The End Of April?____

_____

_____

you don't have
to go fast.
you just have
to GO.

APRIL 1, 20____

About Today: _____

_____

_____

_____

You're Grateful For: _____

Your Happiest Moment Was: _____

_____

_____

What Inspires You? _____

_____

_____

APRIL 1, 20____

About Today: _____

_____

_____

_____

You're Grateful For: _____

Your Happiest Moment Was: _____

_____

_____

What Inspires You? _____

_____

_____

APRIL 2, 20____

About Today: _____

_____

_____

_____

You're Grateful For:_____

Your Happiest Moment Was: _____

_____

_____

How Can You Simplify Your Life? _____

_____

_____

APRIL 2, 20____

About Today: _____

_____

_____

_____

You're Grateful For:_____

Your Happiest Moment Was: _____

_____

_____

How Can You Simplify Your Life? _____

_____

_____

APRIL 3, 20____

About Today: _____

_____

_____

_____

You're Grateful For: _____

Your Happiest Moment Was: _____

_____

_____

Is It More Important To Love Or To Be Loved? _____

_____

_____

APRIL 3, 20____

About Today: _____

_____

_____

_____

You're Grateful For: _____

Your Happiest Moment Was: _____

_____

_____

Is It More Important To Love Or To Be Loved? _____

_____

_____

APRIL 4, 20____

About Today: _____

_____

_____

_____

You're Grateful For:_____

Your Happiest Moment Was: _____

_____

_____

What Are Some Things You've Learned From Your Grandfathers? _____

_____

_____

APRIL 4, 20____

About Today: _____

_____

_____

_____

You're Grateful For:_____

Your Happiest Moment Was: _____

_____

_____

What Are Some Things You've Learned From Your Grandfathers? _____

_____

_____

APRIL 5, 20____

About Today: _____

_____

_____

_____

You're Grateful For: _____

Your Happiest Moment Was: _____

_____

_____

What Are You Good At? _____

_____

_____

APRIL 5, 20____

About Today: _____

_____

_____

_____

You're Grateful For: _____

Your Happiest Moment Was: _____

_____

_____

What Are You Good At? _____

_____

_____

APRIL 6, 20____

About Today: _____

_____

_____

_____

You're Grateful For: _____

Your Happiest Moment Was: _____

_____

_____

Did You Show Compassion Today? _____

_____

_____

APRIL 6, 20____

About Today: _____

_____

_____

_____

You're Grateful For: _____

Your Happiest Moment Was: _____

_____

_____

Did You Show Compassion Today? _____

_____

_____

APRIL 7, 20___

About Today: _____

_____

_____

_____

You're Grateful For: _____

Your Happiest Moment Was: _____

_____

_____

Do You Think It's Too Late To Do Certain Things? If So, Why? _____

_____

_____

APRIL 7, 20___

About Today: _____

_____

_____

_____

You're Grateful For: _____

Your Happiest Moment Was: _____

_____

_____

Do You Think It's Too Late To Do Certain Things? If So, Why? _____

_____

_____

APRIL 8, 20____

About Today: _____
_____
_____
_____

You're Grateful For:_____

Your Happiest Moment Was: _____
_____
_____

If You Could Be An Olympic Athlete, In Which Sport Would You Compete?
_____
_____

APRIL 8, 20____

About Today: _____
_____
_____
_____

You're Grateful For:_____

Your Happiest Moment Was: _____
_____
_____

If You Could Be An Olympic Athlete, In Which Sport Would You Compete?
_____
_____

APRIL 9, 20____

About Today: _____

_____

_____

_____

You're Grateful For: _____

Your Happiest Moment Was: _____

_____

_____

List Three Things You Like About Yourself: _____

_____

_____

APRIL 9, 20____

About Today: _____

_____

_____

_____

You're Grateful For: _____

Your Happiest Moment Was: _____

_____

_____

List Three Things You Like About Yourself: _____

_____

_____

APRIL 10, 20____

About Today: _____

_____

_____

_____

You're Grateful For:_____

Your Happiest Moment Was: _____

_____

_____

List Three More Things You Like About Yourself:_____

_____

_____

APRIL 10, 20____

About Today: _____

_____

_____

_____

You're Grateful For:_____

Your Happiest Moment Was: _____

_____

_____

List Three More Things You Like About Yourself:_____

_____

_____

APRIL 11, 20____

About Today: _____

_____

_____

_____

You're Grateful For: _____

Your Happiest Moment Was: _____

_____

_____

What's A Recent Mistake You Made? _____

_____

_____

APRIL 11, 20____

About Today: _____

_____

_____

_____

You're Grateful For:_____

Your Happiest Moment Was: _____

_____

_____

What's A Recent Mistake You Made?_____

_____

_____

APRIL 12, 20____

About Today: _____

_____

_____

_____

You're Grateful For: _____

Your Happiest Moment Was: _____

_____

_____

How Often Do Your Biggest Fears & Worries Come True? _____

_____

_____

APRIL 12, 20____

About Today: _____

_____

_____

_____

You're Grateful For: _____

Your Happiest Moment Was: _____

_____

_____

How Often Do Your Biggest Fears & Worries Come True? _____

_____

_____

APRIL 13, 20____

About Today: _____

_____

_____

_____

You're Grateful For: _____

Your Happiest Moment Was: _____

_____

_____

When Was The Last Time You Ate Something New? _____

_____

_____

APRIL 13, 20____

About Today: _____

_____

_____

_____

You're Grateful For: _____

Your Happiest Moment Was: _____

_____

_____

When Was The Last Time You Ate Something New? _____

_____

_____

APRIL 14, 20____

About Today: _____
_____
_____
_____

You're Grateful For:_____

Your Happiest Moment Was: _____
_____
_____

What's Something New You've Recently Learned About Your Partner?
_____
_____

APRIL 14, 20____

About Today: _____
_____
_____
_____

You're Grateful For:_____

Your Happiest Moment Was: _____
_____
_____

What's Something New You've Recently Learned About Your Partner?
_____
_____

APRIL 15, 20___

About Today: _____

_____

_____

_____

You're Grateful For: _____

Your Happiest Moment Was: _____

_____

_____

What Does A Meaningful Life Look Like To You? _____

_____

_____

APRIL 15, 20___

About Today: _____

_____

_____

_____

You're Grateful For: _____

Your Happiest Moment Was: _____

_____

What Does A Meaningful Life Look Like To You? _____

_____

APRIL 16, 20____

About Today: _____

_____

_____

_____

You're Grateful For:_____

Your Happiest Moment Was: _____

_____

_____

Did You Make Anyone Smile Today? _____

_____

_____

APRIL 16, 20____

About Today: _____

_____

_____

_____

You're Grateful For:_____

Your Happiest Moment Was: _____

_____

_____

Did You Make Anyone Smile Today? _____

_____

_____

APRIL 17, 20____

About Today: _____

_____

_____

_____

You're Grateful For: _____

Your Happiest Moment Was: _____

_____

_____

What Do You Consider An Ideal Diet? _____

_____

_____

APRIL 17, 20____

About Today: _____

_____

_____

_____

You're Grateful For: _____

Your Happiest Moment Was: _____

_____

_____

What Do You Consider An Ideal Diet? _____

_____

_____

APRIL 18, 20____

About Today: _____

_____

_____

_____

You're Grateful For:_____

Your Happiest Moment Was: _____

_____

_____

What 3 Items Would You Want With You On A Deserted Island?_____

_____

_____

APRIL 18, 20____

About Today: _____

_____

_____

_____

You're Grateful For:_____

Your Happiest Moment Was: _____

_____

_____

What 3 Items Would You Want With You On A Deserted Island?_____

_____

_____

APRIL 19, 20____

About Today: _____

_____

_____

_____

You're Grateful For: _____

Your Happiest Moment Was: _____

_____

_____

Who Inspires You Most? Can You Be More Like Them? _____

_____

_____

APRIL 19, 20____

About Today: _____

_____

_____

_____

You're Grateful For: _____

Your Happiest Moment Was: _____

_____

_____

Who Inspires You Most? Can You Be More Like Them? _____

_____

APRIL 20, 20____

About Today: _____

_____

_____

_____

You're Grateful For: _____

Your Happiest Moment Was: _____

_____

_____

Do You Own Things You Haven't Used In Years? _____

_____

_____

APRIL 20, 20____

About Today: _____

_____

_____

_____

You're Grateful For: _____

Your Happiest Moment Was: _____

_____

_____

Do You Own Things You Haven't Used In Years? _____

_____

_____

APRIL 21, 20____

About Today: _____

_____

_____

_____

You're Grateful For:_____

Your Happiest Moment Was: _____

_____

_____

How Does Being Naked Make You Feel?_____

_____

_____

APRIL 21, 20____

About Today: _____

_____

_____

_____

You're Grateful For:_____

Your Happiest Moment Was: _____

_____

_____

How Does Being Naked Make You Feel?_____

_____

_____

APRIL 22, 20____

About Today: _____
_____
_____
_____

You're Grateful For:_____

Your Happiest Moment Was: _____
_____
_____

What's Most Important To You In Life? _____
_____
_____

APRIL 22, 20____

About Today: _____
_____
_____
_____

You're Grateful For:_____

Your Happiest Moment Was: _____
_____
_____

What's Most Important To You In Life? _____
_____
_____

APRIL 23, 20____

About Today: _____

_____

_____

_____

You're Grateful For: _____

Your Happiest Moment Was: _____

_____

_____

Where Would You Prefer To Live: City, Coast, Mountains, Country, etc.?

_____

_____

APRIL 23, 20____

About Today: _____

_____

_____

_____

You're Grateful For: _____

Your Happiest Moment Was: _____

_____

_____

Where Would You Prefer To Live: City, Coast, Mountains, Country, etc.?

_____

_____

APRIL 24, 20____

About Today: _____

_____

_____

_____

You're Grateful For:_____

Your Happiest Moment Was: _____

_____

_____

What's One Of Your Fondest Childhood Memories? _____

_____

_____

APRIL 24, 20____

About Today: _____

_____

_____

_____

You're Grateful For:_____

Your Happiest Moment Was: _____

_____

_____

What's One Of Your Fondest Childhood Memories? _____

_____

_____

APRIL 25, 20____

About Today: _____

_____

_____

_____

You're Grateful For: _____

Your Happiest Moment Was: _____

_____

_____

Do You Consider Yourself A Likable Person? _____

_____

_____

APRIL 25, 20____

About Today: _____

_____

_____

_____

You're Grateful For: _____

Your Happiest Moment Was: _____

_____

_____

Do You Consider Yourself A Likable Person? _____

_____

_____

APRIL 26, 20____

About Today: _____

_____

_____

_____

You're Grateful For:_____

Your Happiest Moment Was: _____

_____

_____

Did Anything Frighten You Today? _____

_____

_____

APRIL 26, 20____

About Today: _____

_____

_____

_____

You're Grateful For:_____

Your Happiest Moment Was: _____

_____

_____

Did Anything Frighten You Today? _____

_____

_____

APRIL 27, 20___

About Today: _____

_____

_____

_____

You're Grateful For: _____

Your Happiest Moment Was: _____

_____

_____

List Five Things You Need From A Partner: _____

_____

_____

APRIL 27, 20___

About Today: _____

_____

_____

_____

You're Grateful For: _____

Your Happiest Moment Was: _____

_____

_____

List Five Things You Need From A Partner: _____

_____

_____

APRIL 28, 20____

About Today: _____

_____

_____

_____

You're Grateful For:_____

Your Happiest Moment Was:_____

_____

_____

How Often Do You Go To Bed Angry? _____

_____

_____

APRIL 28, 20____

About Today: _____

_____

_____

_____

You're Grateful For:_____

Your Happiest Moment Was:_____

_____

_____

How Often Do You Go To Bed Angry? _____

_____

_____

APRIL 29, 20____

About Today: _____

_____

_____

_____

You're Grateful For: _____

Your Happiest Moment Was: _____

_____

_____

Another Month Has Gone. Are You Closer To Living The Life You Want?

_____

_____

APRIL 29, 20____

About Today: _____

_____

_____

_____

You're Grateful For: _____

Your Happiest Moment Was: _____

_____

_____

Another Month Has Gone. Are You Closer To Living The Life You Want?

_____

_____

APRIL 30, 20____

About Today: _____

_____

_____

_____

You're Grateful For:_____

Your Happiest Moment Was: _____

_____

_____

What Do You Want To Accomplish By The End Of May?_____

_____

_____

APRIL 30, 20____

About Today: _____

_____

_____

_____

You're Grateful For:_____

Your Happiest Moment Was: _____

_____

_____

What Do You Want To Accomplish By The End Of May?_____

_____

_____

Document the moments you feel most in love with yourself - what you're wearing, who you're around, what you're doing. Recreate and repeat.

-WARSAN SHIRE

MAY 1, 20____

About Today: _____

_____

_____

_____

You're Grateful For:_____

Your Happiest Moment Was: _____

_____

_____

How Do Rainy Days Make You Feel?_____

_____

_____

MAY 1, 20____

About Today: _____

_____

_____

_____

You're Grateful For:_____

Your Happiest Moment Was: _____

_____

_____

How Do Rainy Days Make You Feel? _____

_____

_____

MAY 2, 20____

About Today: _____

_____

_____

_____

You're Grateful For: _____

Your Happiest Moment Was: _____

_____

_____

How Does Your Partner Demonstrate Love? _____

_____

_____

MAY 2, 20____

About Today: _____

_____

_____

_____

You're Grateful For: _____

Your Happiest Moment Was: _____

_____

_____

How Does Your Partner Demonstrate Love? _____

_____

_____

MAY 3, 20____

About Today: _____

_____

_____

_____

You're Grateful For: _____

Your Happiest Moment Was: _____

_____

_____

How Many Friends Can You Trust With A Secret? _____

_____

_____

MAY 3, 20____

About Today: _____

_____

_____

_____

You're Grateful For: _____

Your Happiest Moment Was: _____

_____

_____

How Many Friends Can You Trust With A Secret? _____

_____

_____

MAY 4, 20____

About Today: _____

_____

_____

_____

You're Grateful For:_____

Your Happiest Moment Was: _____

_____

_____

When You Have A Bad Day, How Do You Practice Self-Care? _____

_____

_____

MAY 4, 20____

About Today: _____

_____

_____

_____

You're Grateful For:_____

Your Happiest Moment Was: _____

_____

_____

When You Have A Bad Day, How Do You Practice Self-Care? _____

_____

MAY 5, 20____

About Today: _____

_____

_____

_____

You're Grateful For:_____

Your Happiest Moment Was: _____

_____

_____

Did You Look In A Mirror Today & Like What You Saw? _____

_____

_____

MAY 5, 20____

About Today: _____

_____

_____

_____

You're Grateful For:_____

Your Happiest Moment Was: _____

_____

_____

Did You Look In A Mirror Today & Like What You Saw? _____

_____

_____

MAY 6, 20____

About Today: _____

_____

_____

_____

You're Grateful For: _____

Your Happiest Moment Was: _____

_____

_____

Are You Giving Your Goals The Time They Deserve? _____

_____

_____

MAY 6, 20____

About Today: _____

_____

_____

_____

You're Grateful For: _____

Your Happiest Moment Was: _____

_____

_____

Are You Giving Your Goals The Time They Deserve? _____

_____

MAY 7, 20____

About Today: _____

_____

_____

_____

You're Grateful For:_____

Your Happiest Moment Was: _____

_____

_____

How Important To You Is Down Time? _____

_____

_____

MAY 7, 20____

About Today: _____

_____

_____

_____

You're Grateful For:_____

Your Happiest Moment Was: _____

_____

_____

How Important To You Is Down Time? _____

_____

_____

MAY 8, 20____

About Today: _____

_____

_____

_____

You're Grateful For: _____

Your Happiest Moment Was: _____

_____

_____

What Are Your Favorite Scents? _____

_____

_____

MAY 8, 20____

About Today: _____

_____

_____

_____

You're Grateful For: _____

Your Happiest Moment Was: _____

_____

_____

What Are Your Favorite Scents? _____

_____

_____

MAY 9, 20____

About Today: _____

_____

_____

_____

You're Grateful For: _____

Your Happiest Moment Was: _____

_____

_____

Do You Own Anything That Belongs To The Person You Used To Be?

_____

_____

MAY 9, 20____

About Today: _____

_____

_____

_____

You're Grateful For: _____

Your Happiest Moment Was: _____

_____

_____

Do You Own Anything That Belongs To The Person You Used To Be?

_____

_____

MAY 10, 20___

About Today: _____

_____

_____

_____

You're Grateful For:_____

Your Happiest Moment Was: _____

_____

_____

What's The Difference Between Living & Being Alive?_____

_____

_____

MAY 10, 20___

About Today: _____

_____

_____

_____

You're Grateful For:_____

Your Happiest Moment Was: _____

_____

_____

What's The Difference Between Living & Being Alive?_____

_____

MAY 11, 20____

About Today: _____

_____

_____

_____

You're Grateful For:_____

Your Happiest Moment Was: _____

_____

_____

In One Word, What's Standing Between You & Your Biggest Goal?

_____

_____

MAY 11, 20____

About Today: _____

_____

_____

_____

You're Grateful For:_____

Your Happiest Moment Was: _____

_____

In One Word, What's Standing Between You & Your Biggest Goal?

_____

_____

MAY 12, 20____

About Today: _____

_____

_____

_____

You're Grateful For: _____

Your Happiest Moment Was: _____

_____

_____

If One Wish Could Be Granted, What Would You Wish *For Yourself*?

_____

_____

MAY 12, 20____

About Today: _____

_____

_____

_____

You're Grateful For: _____

Your Happiest Moment Was: _____

_____

_____

If One Wish Could Be Granted, What Would You Wish *For Yourself*?

_____

_____

MAY 13, 20____

About Today: _____

_____

_____

_____

You're Grateful For: _____

Your Happiest Moment Was: _____

_____

_____

Which Five People Do You Spend The Most Time With? _____

_____

_____

MAY 13, 20____

About Today: _____

_____

_____

_____

You're Grateful For: _____

Your Happiest Moment Was: _____

_____

Which Five People Do You Spend The Most Time With? _____

_____

_____

MAY 14, 20____

About Today: _____

_____

_____

_____

You're Grateful For: _____

Your Happiest Moment Was: _____

_____

_____

Do You Like Your Hair Style? If Not, What's Stopping You From Changing It?

_____

_____

MAY 14, 20____

About Today: _____

_____

_____

_____

You're Grateful For: _____

Your Happiest Moment Was: _____

_____

_____

Do You Like Your Hair Style? If Not, What's Stopping You From Changing It?

_____

_____

MAY 15, 20____

About Today: _____

_____

_____

_____

You're Grateful For:_____

Your Happiest Moment Was: _____

_____

_____

What Did You Eat Today? Could You Have Made Better Choices? _____

_____

_____

MAY 15, 20____

About Today: _____

_____

_____

_____

You're Grateful For:_____

Your Happiest Moment Was: _____

_____

_____

What Did You Eat Today? Could You Have Made Better Choices? _____

_____

_____

MAY 16, 20____

About Today: _____

_____

_____

_____

You're Grateful For: _____

Your Happiest Moment Was: _____

_____

_____

Before I Die I Want To: _____

_____

_____

MAY 16, 20____

About Today: _____

_____

_____

_____

You're Grateful For: _____

Your Happiest Moment Was: _____

_____

_____

Before I Die I Want To: _____

_____

_____

MAY 17, 20____

About Today: _____

_____

_____

_____

You're Grateful For: _____

Your Happiest Moment Was: _____

_____

_____

What Stresses You Out? _____

_____

_____

MAY 17, 20____

About Today: _____

_____

_____

_____

You're Grateful For: _____

Your Happiest Moment Was: _____

_____

_____

What Stresses You Out? _____

_____

_____

MAY 18, 20____

About Today: _____

_____

_____

_____

You're Grateful For: _____

Your Happiest Moment Was: _____

_____

_____

What Is The Scariest Thing You've Ever Done? _____

_____

_____

MAY 18, 20____

About Today: _____

_____

_____

_____

You're Grateful For: _____

Your Happiest Moment Was: _____

_____

_____

What Is The Scariest Thing You've Ever Done? _____

_____

_____

MAY 19, 20____

About Today: _____

_____

_____

_____

You're Grateful For:_____

Your Happiest Moment Was: _____

_____

_____

If One Wish Could Be Granted, What Would You Wish *For Humanity?*

_____

_____

MAY 19, 20____

About Today: _____

_____

_____

_____

You're Grateful For:_____

Your Happiest Moment Was: _____

_____

_____

If One Wish Could Be Granted, What Would You Wish *For Humanity?*

_____

_____

MAY 20, 20____

About Today: _____

_____

_____

_____

You're Grateful For: _____

Your Happiest Moment Was: _____

_____

_____

What Artistic Mediums Do You Use To Express Yourself (*Paint, Food, Film, Words, Gardening, etc.*)? _____

_____

MAY 20, 20____

About Today: _____

_____

_____

_____

You're Grateful For: _____

Your Happiest Moment Was: _____

_____

_____

What Artistic Mediums Do You Use To Express Yourself (*Paint, Food, Film, Words, Gardening, etc.*)? _____

_____

MAY 21, 20____

About Today: _____

_____

_____

_____

You're Grateful For: _____

Your Happiest Moment Was: _____

_____

_____

What Are You Sentimental About? _____

_____

_____

MAY 21, 20____

About Today: _____

_____

_____

_____

You're Grateful For: _____

Your Happiest Moment Was: _____

_____

_____

What Are You Sentimental About? _____

_____

_____

MAY 22, 20___

About Today: _____

_____

_____

_____

You're Grateful For: _____

Your Happiest Moment Was: _____

_____

_____

How Do You Demonstrate Your Love? _____

_____

_____

MAY 22, 20___

About Today: _____

_____

_____

_____

You're Grateful For: _____

Your Happiest Moment Was: _____

_____

_____

How Do You Demonstrate Your Love? _____

_____

_____

MAY 23, 20____

About Today: _____

_____

_____

_____

You're Grateful For:_____

Your Happiest Moment Was: _____

_____

_____

If You Could Restore One Broken Relationship, Which Would It Be?

_____

_____

MAY 23, 20____

About Today: _____

_____

_____

_____

You're Grateful For:_____

Your Happiest Moment Was: _____

_____

_____

If You Could Restore One Broken Relationship, Which Would It Be?

_____

_____

MAY 24, 20____

About Today: _____

_____

_____

_____

You're Grateful For: _____

Your Happiest Moment Was: _____

_____

_____

Where Do You Find Peace? _____

_____

_____

MAY 24, 20____

About Today: _____

_____

_____

_____

You're Grateful For: _____

Your Happiest Moment Was: _____

_____

_____

Where Do You Find Peace? _____

_____

_____

MAY 25, 20____

About Today: _____

_____

_____

_____

You're Grateful For: _____

Your Happiest Moment Was: _____

_____

_____

Were You Unkind Today? To Whom? Can You Apologize? _____

_____

_____

MAY 25, 20____

About Today: _____

_____

_____

_____

You're Grateful For: _____

Your Happiest Moment Was: _____

_____

_____

Were You Unkind Today? To Whom? Can You Apologize? _____

_____

_____

MAY 26, 20____

About Today: _____
_____
_____
_____

You're Grateful For: _____

Your Happiest Moment Was: _____
_____
_____

What Risk Would You Take If You Knew You Couldn't Fail? _____
_____
_____

MAY 26, 20____

About Today: _____
_____
_____
_____

You're Grateful For: _____

Your Happiest Moment Was: _____
_____
_____

What Risk Would You Take If You Knew You Couldn't Fail? _____
_____
_____

MAY 27, 20____

About Today: _____

_____

_____

_____

You're Grateful For:_____

Your Happiest Moment Was: _____

_____

_____

How Old Do You Feel Today?_____

_____

_____

MAY 27, 20____

About Today: _____

_____

_____

You're Grateful For:_____

Your Happiest Moment Was: _____

_____

_____

How Old Do You Feel Today? _____

_____

_____

MAY 28, 20____

About Today: _____

_____

_____

_____

You're Grateful For: _____

Your Happiest Moment Was: _____

_____

_____

What Did You Want To Be When You Grew Up? _____

_____

_____

MAY 28, 20____

About Today: _____

_____

_____

_____

You're Grateful For: _____

Your Happiest Moment Was: _____

_____

_____

What Did You Want To Be When You Grew Up? _____

_____

_____

MAY 29, 20____

About Today: _____

_____

_____

_____

You're Grateful For:_____

Your Happiest Moment Was: _____

_____

_____

Do You Consider Yourself A Generous Person? _____

_____

_____

MAY 29, 20____

About Today: _____

_____

_____

_____

You're Grateful For:_____

Your Happiest Moment Was: _____

_____

_____

Do You Consider Yourself A Generous Person? _____

_____

_____

MAY 30, 20____

About Today: _____

_____

_____

_____

You're Grateful For: _____

Your Happiest Moment Was: _____

_____

_____

Another Month Has Gone. Are You Excited For What The Future Will Bring?

_____

_____

MAY 30, 20____

About Today: _____

_____

_____

_____

You're Grateful For: _____

Your Happiest Moment Was: _____

_____

_____

Another Month Has Gone. Are You Excited For What The Future Will Bring?

_____

_____

MAY 31, 20____

About Today: _____
_____
_____
_____

You're Grateful For:_____

Your Happiest Moment Was: _____
_____
_____

What Do You Want To Accomplish By The End Of June?_____
_____
_____

MAY 31, 20____

About Today: _____
_____
_____
_____

You're Grateful For:_____

Your Happiest Moment Was: _____
_____
_____

What Do You Want To Accomplish By The End Of June?_____
_____
_____

Don't promise when you're happy. Don't reply when you're angry. Don't decide when you're sad.

JUNE 1, 20____

About Today: _____

_____

_____

_____

You're Grateful For:_____

Your Happiest Moment Was: _____

_____

_____

What Have You Always Wanted To Do, But Haven't Yet? _____

_____

_____

JUNE 1, 20____

About Today: _____

_____

_____

_____

You're Grateful For:_____

Your Happiest Moment Was: _____

_____

_____

What Have You Always Wanted To Do, But Haven't Yet? _____

_____

_____

JUNE 2, 20___

About Today: _____

_____

_____

_____

You're Grateful For: _____

Your Happiest Moment Was: _____

_____

_____

Does Everyone Deserve Forgiveness? _____

_____

_____

JUNE 2, 20___

About Today: _____

_____

_____

_____

You're Grateful For: _____

Your Happiest Moment Was: _____

_____

_____

Does Everyone Deserve Forgiveness? _____

_____

_____

JUNE 3, 20____

About Today: _____

_____

_____

_____

You're Grateful For: _____

Your Happiest Moment Was: _____

_____

_____

If One Wish Could Be Granted, What Would You Wish *For Someone Else*?

_____

_____

JUNE 3, 20____

About Today: _____

_____

_____

_____

You're Grateful For: _____

Your Happiest Moment Was: _____

_____

_____

If One Wish Could Be Granted, What Would You Wish *For Someone Else*?

_____

_____

JUNE 4, 20____

About Today: _____

_____

_____

_____

You're Grateful For: _____

Your Happiest Moment Was: _____

_____

_____

What Permission Do You Need/Want In Order To Move Forward? _____

_____

_____

JUNE 4, 20____

About Today: _____

_____

_____

_____

You're Grateful For: _____

Your Happiest Moment Was: _____

_____

_____

What Permission Do You Need/Want In Order To Move Forward? _____

_____

JUNE 5, 20___

About Today: _____

_____

_____

_____

You're Grateful For: _____

Your Happiest Moment Was: _____

_____

_____

Did You Get Rid Of Anything Today? _____

_____

_____

JUNE 5, 20___

About Today: _____

_____

_____

_____

You're Grateful For: _____

Your Happiest Moment Was: _____

_____

_____

Did You Get Rid Of Anything Today? _____

_____

_____

JUNE 6, 20____

About Today: _____

_____

_____

_____

You're Grateful For: _____

Your Happiest Moment Was: _____

_____

_____

What Might Your Friends & Family Define As Your Weaknesses?

_____

_____

JUNE 6, 20____

About Today: _____

_____

_____

_____

You're Grateful For: _____

Your Happiest Moment Was: _____

_____

_____

What Might Your Friends & Family Define As Your Weaknesses?

_____

_____

JUNE 7, 20____

About Today: _____

_____

_____

_____

You're Grateful For:_____

Your Happiest Moment Was: _____

_____

_____

What Are Your Recurring Daydreams? _____

_____

_____

JUNE 7, 20____

About Today: _____

_____

_____

_____

You're Grateful For:_____

Your Happiest Moment Was: _____

_____

_____

What Are Your Recurring Daydreams? _____

_____

_____

JUNE 8, 20____

About Today: _____

_____

_____

_____

You're Grateful For: _____

Your Happiest Moment Was: _____

_____

_____

How Do You Recharge? _____

_____

_____

JUNE 8, 20____

About Today: _____

_____

_____

_____

You're Grateful For: _____

Your Happiest Moment Was: _____

_____

_____

How Do You Recharge? _____

_____

_____

JUNE 9, 20___

About Today: _____

_____

_____

_____

You're Grateful For:_____

Your Happiest Moment Was: _____

_____

_____

Did Anyone Tell You They Love You Today? Who? _____

_____

_____

JUNE 9, 20___

About Today: _____

_____

_____

_____

You're Grateful For:_____

Your Happiest Moment Was: _____

_____

_____

Did Anyone Tell You They Love You Today? Who? _____

_____

_____

JUNE 10, 20____

About Today: _____

_____

_____

_____

You're Grateful For:_____

Your Happiest Moment Was: _____

_____

_____

What Accomplishment Are You Most Proud Of? _____

_____

_____

JUNE 10, 20____

About Today: _____

_____

_____

_____

You're Grateful For:_____

Your Happiest Moment Was: _____

_____

_____

What Accomplishment Are You Most Proud Of? _____

_____

_____

JUNE 11, 20____

About Today: _____

_____

_____

_____

You're Grateful For: _____

Your Happiest Moment Was: _____

_____

_____

What's Your Ideal Life Partner Like? _____

_____

_____

JUNE 11, 20____

About Today: _____

_____

_____

_____

You're Grateful For: _____

Your Happiest Moment Was: _____

_____

What's Your Ideal Life Partner Like? _____

_____

_____

JUNE 12, 20____

About Today: _____

_____

_____

_____

You're Grateful For: _____

Your Happiest Moment Was: _____

_____

_____

What's The Most Spontaneous Thing You've Ever Done? _____

_____

_____

JUNE 12, 20____

About Today: _____

_____

_____

_____

You're Grateful For: _____

Your Happiest Moment Was: _____

_____

_____

What's The Most Spontaneous Thing You've Ever Done? _____

_____

_____

JUNE 13, 20___

About Today: _____

_____

_____

_____

You're Grateful For:_____

Your Happiest Moment Was: _____

_____

_____

When Did You Last Laugh So Much It Hurt? _____

_____

_____

JUNE 13, 20___

About Today: _____

_____

_____

_____

You're Grateful For:_____

Your Happiest Moment Was: _____

_____

_____

When Did You Last Laugh So Much It Hurt? _____

_____

_____

JUNE 14, 20____

About Today: _____

_____

_____

_____

You're Grateful For: _____

Your Happiest Moment Was: _____

_____

_____

How Are You Not Accepting Of Your Partner For Who They Really Are?

_____

_____

JUNE 14, 20____

About Today: _____

_____

_____

_____

You're Grateful For: _____

Your Happiest Moment Was: _____

_____

How Are You Not Accepting Of Your Partner For Who They Really Are?

_____

_____

JUNE 15, 20____

About Today: _____

_____

_____

_____

You're Grateful For:_____

Your Happiest Moment Was: _____

_____

_____

What Could You Have Done Better Today? _____

_____

_____

JUNE 15, 20____

About Today: _____

_____

_____

_____

You're Grateful For:_____

Your Happiest Moment Was: _____

_____

_____

What Could You Have Done Better Today? _____

_____

_____

JUNE 16, 20____

About Today: _____

_____

_____

_____

You're Grateful For: _____

Your Happiest Moment Was: _____

_____

_____

What Amazes You? _____

_____

_____

JUNE 16, 20____

About Today: _____

_____

_____

_____

You're Grateful For: _____

Your Happiest Moment Was: _____

_____

What Amazes You? _____

_____

_____

JUNE 17, 20____

About Today: _____

_____

_____

_____

You're Grateful For:_____

Your Happiest Moment Was: _____

_____

_____

What's Worrying You? Will It Matter In 5 Days? 5 Weeks?_____

_____

_____

JUNE 17, 20____

About Today: _____

_____

_____

_____

You're Grateful For:_____

Your Happiest Moment Was: _____

_____

_____

What's Worrying You? Will It Matter In 5 Days? 5 Weeks? _____

_____

_____

JUNE 18, 20____

About Today: _____

_____

_____

_____

You're Grateful For: _____

Your Happiest Moment Was: _____

_____

_____

If You Could Travel One Year Ahead, What Would You Tell Your Future-Self?

_____

_____

JUNE 18, 20____

About Today: _____

_____

_____

_____

You're Grateful For: _____

Your Happiest Moment Was: _____

_____

_____

If You Could Travel One Year Ahead, What Would You Tell Your Future-Self?

_____

_____

JUNE 19, 20___

About Today: _____

_____

_____

_____

You're Grateful For:_____

Your Happiest Moment Was: _____

_____

_____

What's The Last Homemade Thing You Cooked Or Baked? How Did It Taste?

_____

_____

JUNE 19, 20___

About Today: _____

_____

_____

_____

You're Grateful For:_____

Your Happiest Moment Was: _____

_____

_____

What's The Last Homemade Thing You Cooked Or Baked? How Did It Taste?

_____

_____

JUNE 20, 20___

About Today: _____
_____
_____
_____

You're Grateful For:_____

Your Happiest Moment Was: _____
_____
_____

If You Could Eliminate One Thing From Your Life, What Would It Be?
_____
_____

JUNE 20, 20___

About Today: _____
_____
_____
_____

You're Grateful For:_____

Your Happiest Moment Was: _____
_____
_____

If You Could Eliminate One Thing From Your Life, What Would It Be?
_____
_____

JUNE 21, 20___

About Today: _____

_____

_____

_____

You're Grateful For: _____

Your Happiest Moment Was: _____

_____

_____

What Does It Mean To Be Your *Best Self*? _____

_____

_____

JUNE 21, 20___

About Today: _____

_____

_____

_____

You're Grateful For: _____

Your Happiest Moment Was: _____

_____

_____

What Does It Mean To Be Your *Best Self*? _____

_____

_____

JUNE 22, 20___

About Today: _____

_____

_____

_____

You're Grateful For: _____

Your Happiest Moment Was: _____

_____

_____

What Good Habits Do You Want To Cultivate? _____

_____

_____

JUNE 22, 20___

About Today: _____

_____

_____

_____

You're Grateful For: _____

Your Happiest Moment Was: _____

_____

_____

What Good Habits Do You Want To Cultivate? _____

_____

_____

JUNE 23, 20____

About Today: _____

_____

_____

_____

You're Grateful For: _____

Your Happiest Moment Was: _____

_____

_____

What's Your Favorite Book & Why Does It Speak To You? _____

_____

_____

JUNE 23, 20____

About Today: _____

_____

_____

_____

You're Grateful For: _____

Your Happiest Moment Was: _____

_____

_____

What's Your Favorite Book & Why Does It Speak To You? _____

_____

_____

JUNE 24, 20____

About Today: _____

_____

_____

_____

You're Grateful For:_____

Your Happiest Moment Was: _____

_____

_____

What's The Most Valuable Thing You've Learned From An Older Sibling?

_____

_____

JUNE 24, 20____

About Today: _____

_____

_____

_____

You're Grateful For:_____

Your Happiest Moment Was: _____

_____

_____

What's The Most Valuable Thing You've Learned From An Older Sibling?

_____

_____

JUNE 25, 20___

About Today: _____
_____
_____
_____

You're Grateful For:_____

Your Happiest Moment Was:_____
_____
_____

Why Do You Matter? _____
_____

JUNE 25, 20___

About Today: _____
_____
_____
_____

You're Grateful For:_____

Your Happiest Moment Was:_____
_____

Why Do You Matter? _____
_____
_____

JUNE 26, 20____

About Today: _____

_____

_____

_____

You're Grateful For: _____

Your Happiest Moment Was: _____

_____

_____

How Can You Bring More Joy Into Your Life Today? _____

_____

JUNE 26, 20____

About Today: _____

_____

_____

_____

You're Grateful For: _____

Your Happiest Moment Was: _____

_____

How Can You Bring More Joy Into Your Life Today? _____

_____

JUNE 27, 20____

About Today: _____

_____

_____

_____

You're Grateful For:_____

Your Happiest Moment Was:_____

_____

_____

Does Your Career Align With Your Core Values?_____

_____

JUNE 27, 20____

About Today: _____

_____

_____

_____

You're Grateful For:_____

Your Happiest Moment Was:_____

_____

_____

Does Your Career Align With Your Core Values?_____

_____

_____

JUNE 28, 20____

About Today: _____

_____

_____

_____

You're Grateful For: _____

Your Happiest Moment Was: _____

_____

_____

Is There Something You've Been Unable To Forgive Yourself For? _____

_____

_____

JUNE 28, 20____

About Today: _____

_____

_____

_____

You're Grateful For: _____

Your Happiest Moment Was: _____

_____

_____

Is There Something You've Been Unable To Forgive Yourself For? _____

_____

_____

JUNE 29, 20____

About Today: _____

_____

_____

_____

You're Grateful For:_____

Your Happiest Moment Was:_____

_____

_____

Half A Year Has Gone. What Adjustments Should You Make To End It Strong?

_____

_____

JUNE 29, 20____

About Today: _____

_____

_____

_____

You're Grateful For:_____

Your Happiest Moment Was:_____

_____

_____

Half A Year Has Gone. What Adjustments Should You Make To End It Strong?

_____

_____

JUNE 30, 20___

About Today: _____

_____

_____

_____

You're Grateful For: _____

Your Happiest Moment Was: _____

_____

_____

What Do You Want To Accomplish By The End Of July? _____

_____

_____

JUNE 30, 20___

About Today: _____

_____

_____

_____

You're Grateful For: _____

Your Happiest Moment Was: _____

_____

_____

What Do You Want To Accomplish By The End Of July? _____

_____

_____

TAKE TIME TO DO
WHAT MAKES
YOUR SOUL
HAPPY

JULY 1, 20____

About Today: _____

_____

_____

_____

You're Grateful For: _____

Your Happiest Moment Was: _____

_____

_____

When Was The Last Time You Felt Creative? _____

_____

_____

JULY 1, 20____

About Today: _____

_____

_____

_____

You're Grateful For: _____

Your Happiest Moment Was: _____

_____

_____

When Was The Last Time You Felt Creative? _____

_____

_____

JULY 2, 20___

About Today: _____

_____

_____

_____

You're Grateful For:_____

Your Happiest Moment Was: _____

_____

_____

Is Your Life Complicated By Unnecessary Things? _____

_____

_____

JULY 2, 20___

About Today: _____

_____

_____

_____

You're Grateful For:_____

Your Happiest Moment Was: _____

_____

_____

Is Your Life Complicated By Unnecessary Things? _____

_____

_____

JULY 3, 20____

About Today: _____

_____

_____

_____

You're Grateful For: _____

Your Happiest Moment Was: _____

_____

_____

What's One Of The Nicest Things Someone's Ever Done For You? _____

_____

_____

JULY 3, 20____

About Today: _____

_____

_____

_____

You're Grateful For: _____

Your Happiest Moment Was: _____

_____

_____

What's One Of The Nicest Things Someone's Ever Done For You? _____

_____

_____

JULY 4, 20____

About Today: _____

_____

_____

_____

You're Grateful For: _____

Your Happiest Moment Was: _____

_____

_____

What's *Home* To You? Where Is It? _____

_____

_____

JULY 4, 20____

About Today: _____

_____

_____

_____

You're Grateful For: _____

Your Happiest Moment Was: _____

_____

_____

What's *Home* To You? Where Is It? _____

_____

_____

JULY 5, 20____

About Today: _____

_____

_____

_____

You're Grateful For:_____

Your Happiest Moment Was: _____

_____

_____

What Was Your Favorite Summer Activity As A Child?_____

_____

_____

JULY 5, 20____

About Today: _____

_____

_____

_____

You're Grateful For:_____

Your Happiest Moment Was: _____

_____

What Was Your Favorite Summer Activity As A Child?_____

_____

_____

JULY 6, 20____

About Today: _____

_____

_____

_____

You're Grateful For: _____

Your Happiest Moment Was: _____

_____

_____

Are You Living A Meaningful Life? _____

_____

_____

JULY 6, 20____

About Today: _____

_____

_____

_____

You're Grateful For: _____

Your Happiest Moment Was: _____

_____

Are You Living A Meaningful Life? _____

_____

_____

JULY 7, 20____

About Today: _____

_____

_____

_____

You're Grateful For: _____

Your Happiest Moment Was: _____

_____

_____

Did You Feel Disappointment Today? Why? _____

_____

_____

JULY 7, 20____

About Today: _____

_____

_____

_____

You're Grateful For: _____

Your Happiest Moment Was: _____

_____

_____

Did You Feel Disappointment Today? Why? _____

_____

_____

JULY 8, 20____

About Today: _____

_____

_____

_____

You're Grateful For: _____

Your Happiest Moment Was: _____

_____

_____

What Do You Love Most About Your Mother? Does/Did She Know?

_____

_____

JULY 8, 20____

About Today: _____

_____

_____

_____

You're Grateful For: _____

Your Happiest Moment Was: _____

_____

_____

What Do You Love Most About Your Mother? Does/Did She Know?

_____

_____

JULY 9, 20____

About Today: _____

_____

_____

_____

You're Grateful For: _____

Your Happiest Moment Was: _____

_____

_____

Is Your Life Well-Balanced Between Work & Play? _____

_____

_____

JULY 9, 20____

About Today: _____

_____

_____

_____

You're Grateful For: _____

Your Happiest Moment Was: _____

_____

_____

Is Your Life Well-Balanced Between Work & Play? _____

_____

_____

JULY 10, 20____

About Today: _____

_____

_____

_____

You're Grateful For:_____

Your Happiest Moment Was: _____

_____

_____

Are You Afraid Of Getting Close To People? If So, Why? _____

_____

JULY 10, 20____

About Today: _____

_____

_____

_____

You're Grateful For:_____

Your Happiest Moment Was: _____

_____

_____

Are You Afraid Of Getting Close To People? If So, Why? _____

_____

_____

JULY 11, 20____

About Today: _____

_____

_____

_____

You're Grateful For:_____

Your Happiest Moment Was: _____

_____

_____

What Do You Enjoy Doing Over & Over Again? _____

_____

_____

JULY 11, 20____

About Today: _____

_____

_____

_____

You're Grateful For:_____

Your Happiest Moment Was: _____

_____

_____

What Do You Enjoy Doing Over & Over Again? _____

_____

_____

JULY 12, 20____

About Today: _____

_____

_____

_____

You're Grateful For: _____

Your Happiest Moment Was: _____

_____

_____

What's Your Idea Of A Perfect Vacation? _____

_____

_____

JULY 12, 20____

About Today: _____

_____

_____

_____

You're Grateful For: _____

Your Happiest Moment Was: _____

_____

_____

What's Your Idea Of A Perfect Vacation? _____

_____

_____

JULY 13, 20____

About Today: _____

_____

_____

_____

You're Grateful For: _____

Your Happiest Moment Was: _____

_____

_____

Is There Anything You'd Like To Ask Your Grandmothers? _____

_____

_____

JULY 13, 20____

About Today: _____

_____

_____

_____

You're Grateful For: _____

Your Happiest Moment Was: _____

_____

_____

Is There Anything You'd Like To Ask Your Grandmothers? _____

_____

_____

JULY 14, 20____

About Today: _____

_____

_____

_____

You're Grateful For: _____

Your Happiest Moment Was: _____

_____

_____

What Would Make You Feel More Worthy Of Love, Affection & Respect?

_____

_____

JULY 14, 20____

About Today: _____

_____

_____

_____

You're Grateful For: _____

Your Happiest Moment Was: _____

_____

_____

What Would Make You Feel More Worthy Of Love, Affection & Respect?

_____

_____

JULY 15, 20____

About Today: _____

_____

_____

_____

You're Grateful For: _____

Your Happiest Moment Was: _____

_____

_____

What Should You Do Differently Tomorrow? _____

_____

_____

JULY 15, 20____

About Today: _____

_____

_____

_____

You're Grateful For: _____

Your Happiest Moment Was: _____

_____

_____

What Should You Do Differently Tomorrow? _____

_____

_____

JULY 16, 20___

About Today: _____

_____

_____

_____

You're Grateful For: _____

Your Happiest Moment Was: _____

_____

_____

What's Your Greatest Talent? _____

_____

_____

JULY 16, 20___

About Today: _____

_____

_____

_____

You're Grateful For: _____

Your Happiest Moment Was: _____

_____

_____

What's Your Greatest Talent? _____

_____

_____

JULY 17, 20___

About Today: _____

_____

_____

_____

You're Grateful For: _____

Your Happiest Moment Was: _____

_____

_____

What Percentage Of The Clothes In Your Closet Do You Actually Wear?

_____

_____

JULY 17, 20___

About Today: _____

_____

_____

_____

You're Grateful For: _____

Your Happiest Moment Was: _____

_____

_____

What Percentage Of The Clothes In Your Closet Do You Actually Wear?

_____

_____

JULY 18, 20____

About Today: _____

_____

_____

_____

You're Grateful For: _____

Your Happiest Moment Was: _____

_____

_____

What Makes Life Easier? _____

_____

_____

JULY 18, 20____

About Today: _____

_____

_____

_____

You're Grateful For: _____

Your Happiest Moment Was: _____

_____

_____

What Makes Life Easier? _____

_____

_____

JULY 19, 20____

About Today: _____

_____

_____

_____

You're Grateful For:_____

Your Happiest Moment Was: _____

_____

_____

How Often Do You Speak Your Mind? _____

_____

_____

JULY 19, 20____

About Today: _____

_____

_____

_____

You're Grateful For:_____

Your Happiest Moment Was: _____

_____

_____

How Often Do You Speak Your Mind? _____

_____

_____

JULY 20, 20____

About Today: _____

_____

_____

_____

You're Grateful For: _____

Your Happiest Moment Was: _____

_____

_____

Did You Work Toward Your Goals Today? _____

_____

_____

JULY 20, 20____

About Today: _____

_____

_____

_____

You're Grateful For: _____

Your Happiest Moment Was: _____

_____

_____

Did You Work Toward Your Goals Today? _____

_____

_____

JULY 21, 20__

About Today: Woke up with Marlin, had a great night spending time with him. The more time I spend with him, the more I want to be with him. Had a good day at work. Had a great convo with ahmad. Talked about church, taking Dan to church. how good it feels knowing I'm having a good influence on Dan, looking forward to church. Need to get a bible.

You're Grateful For: my family, my job, ahmad, King, marlin

Your Happiest Moment Was: Hearing ahmad tell me how much of a good influence I am on Dan. Waking up to Marlin kissing me. Coming home after a long day at work.

Is There A Place Nearby You Want To Visit, But Haven't Yet? Arizona, Mexico

JULY 21, 20____

About Today: _____

You're Grateful For: _____

Your Happiest Moment Was: _____

Is There A Place Nearby You Want To Visit, But Haven't Yet? _____

JULY 22, 20____

About Today: _____

_____

_____

_____

You're Grateful For: _____

Your Happiest Moment Was: _____

_____

_____

What Do You Love About The Beach? _____

_____

_____

JULY 22, 20____

About Today: _____

_____

_____

_____

You're Grateful For: _____

Your Happiest Moment Was: _____

_____

_____

What Do You Love About The Beach? _____

_____

_____

JULY 23, 20____

About Today: _____

_____

_____

_____

You're Grateful For: _____

Your Happiest Moment Was: _____

_____

_____

Are You Satisfied With How Often You Have Sex? _____

_____

_____

JULY 23, 20____

About Today: _____

_____

_____

_____

You're Grateful For: _____

Your Happiest Moment Was: _____

_____

_____

Are You Satisfied With How Often You Have Sex? _____

_____

_____

JULY 24, 20____

About Today: _____

_____

_____

_____

You're Grateful For: _____

Your Happiest Moment Was: _____

_____

_____

Who Is The Kindest Person You Know? Why Do You Think So? _____

_____

_____

JULY 24, 20____

About Today: _____

_____

_____

_____

You're Grateful For: _____

Your Happiest Moment Was: _____

_____

_____

Who Is The Kindest Person You Know? Why Do You Think So? _____

_____

_____

JULY 25, 20___

About Today: _____

_____

_____

_____

You're Grateful For: _____

Your Happiest Moment Was: _____

_____

_____

What Could You Pay More Attention To? _____

_____

_____

JULY 25, 20___

About Today: _____

_____

_____

_____

You're Grateful For: _____

Your Happiest Moment Was: _____

_____

_____

What Could You Pay More Attention To? _____

_____

_____

JULY 26, 20____

About Today: _____

_____

_____

_____

You're Grateful For: _____

Your Happiest Moment Was: _____

_____

_____

If You No Longer Had To Work, Would You Continue To Do So? Doing What?

_____

_____

JULY 26, 20____

About Today: _____

_____

_____

_____

You're Grateful For: _____

Your Happiest Moment Was: _____

_____

_____

If You No Longer Had To Work, Would You Continue To Do So? Doing What?

_____

_____

JULY 27, 20____

About Today: _____

_____

_____

_____

You're Grateful For: _____

Your Happiest Moment Was: _____

_____

_____

Are You Afraid Of Being Your True Self Around Others? If So, Why? _____

_____

_____

JULY 27, 20____

About Today: _____

_____

_____

_____

You're Grateful For: _____

Your Happiest Moment Was: _____

_____

_____

Are You Afraid Of Being Your True Self Around Others? If So, Why? _____

_____

_____

JULY 28, 20____

About Today: _____

_____

_____

_____

You're Grateful For: _____

Your Happiest Moment Was: _____

_____

_____

Do You Believe In Destiny? _____

_____

_____

JULY 28, 20____

About Today: _____

_____

_____

_____

You're Grateful For: _____

Your Happiest Moment Was: _____

_____

Do You Believe In Destiny? _____

_____

_____

JULY 29, 20____

About Today: _____

_____

_____

_____

You're Grateful For: _____

Your Happiest Moment Was: _____

_____

_____

Who Could You Pay More Attention To? _____

_____

_____

JULY 29, 20____

About Today: _____

_____

_____

_____

You're Grateful For: _____

Your Happiest Moment Was: _____

_____

_____

Who Could You Pay More Attention To? _____

_____

_____

JULY 30, 20____

About Today: _____

_____

_____

_____

You're Grateful For:_____

Your Happiest Moment Was: _____

_____

_____

Another Month Has Gone. What Should You Not Carry Into Next Month?

_____

_____

JULY 30, 20____

About Today: _____

_____

_____

_____

You're Grateful For:_____

Your Happiest Moment Was: _____

_____

Another Month Has Gone. What Should You Not Carry Into Next Month?

_____

_____

JULY 31, 20____

About Today: _____

_____

_____

_____

You're Grateful For: _____

Your Happiest Moment Was: _____

_____

_____

What Do You Want To Accomplish By The End Of August? _____

_____

_____

JULY 31, 20____

About Today: _____

_____

_____

_____

You're Grateful For: _____

Your Happiest Moment Was: _____

_____

_____

What Do You Want To Accomplish By The End Of August? _____

_____

_____

Every Day
May Not Be Good,
But There Is Something Good
In Every Day.

AUGUST 1, 20____

About Today: _____

_____

_____

_____

You're Grateful For:_____

Your Happiest Moment Was: _____

_____

_____

If You Could Visit Anyone's Home Right Now, Whose Would You Choose?

_____

_____

AUGUST 1, 20____

About Today: _____

_____

_____

_____

You're Grateful For:_____

Your Happiest Moment Was: _____

_____

_____

If You Could Visit Anyone's Home Right Now, Whose Would You Choose?

_____

_____

AUGUST 2, 20____

About Today: _____

_____

_____

_____

You're Grateful For: _____

Your Happiest Moment Was: _____

_____

_____

How Often Do You Use Your Greatest Talent? _____

_____

_____

AUGUST 2, 20____

About Today: _____

_____

_____

_____

You're Grateful For: _____

Your Happiest Moment Was: _____

_____

_____

How Often Do You Use Your Greatest Talent? _____

_____

_____

AUGUST 3, 20____

About Today: _____

_____

_____

_____

You're Grateful For: _____

Your Happiest Moment Was: _____

_____

_____

What's Your Relationship With Money?_____

_____

_____

AUGUST 3, 20____

About Today: _____

_____

_____

_____

You're Grateful For:_____

Your Happiest Moment Was: _____

_____

_____

What's Your Relationship With Money? _____

_____

_____

AUGUST 4, 20____

About Today: _____

_____

_____

_____

You're Grateful For: _____

Your Happiest Moment Was: _____

_____

_____

Describe Your Family Using One Word: _____

_____

_____

AUGUST 4, 20____

About Today: _____

_____

_____

_____

You're Grateful For: _____

Your Happiest Moment Was: _____

_____

_____

Describe Your Family Using One Word: _____

_____

_____

AUGUST 5, 20____

About Today: _____

_____

_____

_____

You're Grateful For: _____

Your Happiest Moment Was: _____

_____

_____

Do You Believe In Coincidence? _____

_____

_____

AUGUST 5, 20____

About Today: _____

_____

_____

_____

You're Grateful For: _____

Your Happiest Moment Was: _____

_____

_____

Do You Believe In Coincidence? _____

_____

_____

AUGUST 6, 20____

About Today: _____

_____

_____

_____

You're Grateful For: _____

Your Happiest Moment Was: _____

_____

_____

Did You Sit In Silence For At Least 5 Minutes Today? If Not, Can You Now?

_____

_____

AUGUST 6, 20____

About Today: _____

_____

_____

_____

You're Grateful For: _____

Your Happiest Moment Was: _____

_____

_____

Did You Sit In Silence For At Least 5 Minutes Today? If Not, Can You Now?

_____

_____

AUGUST 7, 20___

About Today: _____

_____

_____

_____

You're Grateful For: _____

Your Happiest Moment Was: _____

_____

_____

If You Had To Work For Free, What Would You Want To Do? _____

_____

_____

AUGUST 7, 20___

About Today: _____

_____

_____

_____

You're Grateful For: _____

Your Happiest Moment Was: _____

_____

_____

If You Had To Work For Free, What Would You Want To Do? _____

_____

_____

AUGUST 8, 20____

About Today: _____

_____

_____

_____

You're Grateful For: _____

Your Happiest Moment Was: _____

_____

_____

What Are You Looking Forward To This Week? ____

_____

_____

AUGUST 8, 20____

About Today: _____

_____

_____

_____

You're Grateful For: _____

Your Happiest Moment Was: _____

_____

What Are You Looking Forward To This Week? ____

_____

_____

AUGUST 9, 20___

About Today: _____

_____

_____

_____

You're Grateful For: _____

Your Happiest Moment Was: _____

_____

_____

Do You Enjoy Your Own Company? _____

_____

_____

AUGUST 9, 20___

About Today: _____

_____

_____

_____

You're Grateful For: _____

Your Happiest Moment Was: _____

_____

_____

Do You Enjoy Your Own Company? _____

_____

_____

AUGUST 10, 20____

About Today: _____

_____

_____

_____

You're Grateful For: _____

Your Happiest Moment Was: _____

_____

_____

What's Your Greatest Fear? _____

_____

_____

AUGUST 10, 20____

About Today: _____

_____

_____

_____

You're Grateful For: _____

Your Happiest Moment Was: _____

_____

_____

What's Your Greatest Fear? _____

_____

_____

AUGUST 11, 20____

About Today: _____

_____

_____

_____

You're Grateful For: _____

Your Happiest Moment Was: _____

_____

_____

Summer Or Winter? Why? _____

_____

_____

AUGUST 11, 20____

About Today: _____

_____

_____

_____

You're Grateful For: _____

Your Happiest Moment Was: _____

_____

_____

Summer Or Winter? Why? _____

_____

_____

AUGUST 12, 20____

About Today: _____

_____

_____

_____

You're Grateful For: _____

Your Happiest Moment Was: _____

_____

_____

Would You Like To Be Famous? For What & In What Way? _____

_____

_____

AUGUST 12, 20____

About Today: _____

_____

_____

_____

You're Grateful For: _____

Your Happiest Moment Was: _____

_____

_____

Would You Like To Be Famous? For What & In What Way? _____

_____

_____

AUGUST 13, 20____

About Today: _____

_____

_____

_____

You're Grateful For: _____

Your Happiest Moment Was: _____

_____

_____

What's Your Idea Of A Perfect Day? _____

_____

_____

AUGUST 13, 20____

About Today: _____

_____

_____

_____

You're Grateful For: _____

Your Happiest Moment Was: _____

_____

_____

What's Your Idea Of A Perfect Day? _____

_____

_____

AUGUST 14, 20___

About Today: _____

_____

_____

_____

You're Grateful For: _____

Your Happiest Moment Was: _____

_____

_____

When Did You Last Sing? _____

_____

_____

AUGUST 14, 20___

About Today: _____

_____

_____

_____

You're Grateful For: _____

Your Happiest Moment Was: _____

_____

_____

When Did You Last Sing? _____

_____

_____

AUGUST 15, 20___

About Today: _____

_____

_____

_____

You're Grateful For: _____

Your Happiest Moment Was: _____

_____

_____

How Do You Know When You Love Someone? _____

_____

_____

AUGUST 15, 20___

About Today: _____

_____

_____

_____

You're Grateful For: _____

Your Happiest Moment Was: _____

_____

_____

How Do You Know When You Love Someone? _____

_____

_____

AUGUST 16, 20____

About Today: _____

_____

_____

_____

You're Grateful For: _____

Your Happiest Moment Was: _____

_____

_____

What In Your Life Do You Feel Most Grateful For? _____

_____

_____

AUGUST 16, 20____

About Today: _____

_____

_____

_____

You're Grateful For: _____

Your Happiest Moment Was: _____

_____

_____

What In Your Life Do You Feel Most Grateful For? _____

_____

_____

AUGUST 17, 20____

About Today: _____

_____

_____

_____

You're Grateful For:_____

Your Happiest Moment Was: _____

_____

_____

If Your Home Caught Fire, What One Object Would You Save? Why?

_____

_____

AUGUST 17, 20____

About Today: _____

_____

_____

_____

You're Grateful For:_____

Your Happiest Moment Was: _____

_____

_____

If Your Home Caught Fire, What One Object Would You Save? Why?

_____

_____

AUGUST 18, 20____

About Today: _____

_____

_____

_____

You're Grateful For: _____

Your Happiest Moment Was: _____

_____

_____

If You Died Suddenly, What Would You Most Regret Not Having Told Someone?

_____

_____

AUGUST 18, 20____

About Today: _____

_____

_____

_____

You're Grateful For: _____

Your Happiest Moment Was: _____

_____

_____

If You Died Suddenly, What Would You Most Regret Not Having Told Someone?

_____

_____

AUGUST 19, 20____

About Today: _____

_____

_____

_____

You're Grateful For: _____

Your Happiest Moment Was: _____

_____

_____

What Might You Be Wasting Money On? _____

_____

_____

AUGUST 19, 20____

About Today: _____

_____

_____

_____

You're Grateful For: _____

Your Happiest Moment Was: _____

_____

_____

What Might You Be Wasting Money On? _____

_____

_____

AUGUST 20, 20____

About Today: _____

_____

_____

_____

You're Grateful For: _____

Your Happiest Moment Was: _____

_____

_____

What Do You Value Most In A Friendship? _____

_____

_____

AUGUST 20, 20____

About Today: _____

_____

_____

_____

You're Grateful For: _____

Your Happiest Moment Was: _____

_____

_____

What Do You Value Most In A Friendship? _____

_____

_____

AUGUST 21, 20____

About Today: _____

_____

_____

_____

You're Grateful For: _____

Your Happiest Moment Was: _____

_____

_____

How Often Do You Give Without Expecting Anything In Return? _____

_____

_____

AUGUST 21, 20____

About Today: _____

_____

_____

_____

You're Grateful For: _____

Your Happiest Moment Was: _____

_____

_____

How Often Do You Give Without Expecting Anything In Return? _____

_____

_____

AUGUST 22, 20____

About Today: _____

_____

_____

_____

You're Grateful For: _____

Your Happiest Moment Was: _____

_____

_____

How Are You? _____

_____

_____

AUGUST 22, 20____

About Today: _____

_____

_____

_____

You're Grateful For: _____

Your Happiest Moment Was: _____

_____

How Are You? _____

_____

_____

AUGUST 23, 20____

About Today: _____

_____

_____

_____

You're Grateful For: _____

Your Happiest Moment Was: _____

_____

_____

What Do You Want To Have Achieved One Year From Now? _____

_____

_____

AUGUST 23, 20____

About Today: _____

_____

_____

_____

You're Grateful For: _____

Your Happiest Moment Was: _____

_____

_____

What Do You Want To Have Achieved One Year From Now? _____

_____

_____

AUGUST 24, 20____

About Today: _____

_____

_____

_____

You're Grateful For:_____

Your Happiest Moment Was: _____

_____

_____

Which Of Your Personality Traits Has Caused You The Most Trouble?

_____

_____

AUGUST 24, 20____

About Today: _____

_____

_____

_____

You're Grateful For:_____

Your Happiest Moment Was: _____

_____

_____

Which Of Your Personality Traits Has Caused You The Most Trouble?

_____

_____

AUGUST 25, 20____

About Today: _____

_____

_____

_____

You're Grateful For: _____

Your Happiest Moment Was: _____

_____

_____

What's Your Favorite Summer Activity? Did You Do It Yet? _____

_____

_____

AUGUST 25, 20____

About Today: _____

_____

_____

_____

You're Grateful For: _____

Your Happiest Moment Was: _____

_____

_____

What's Your Favorite Summer Activity? Did You Do It Yet? _____

_____

_____

AUGUST 26, 20____

About Today: _____

_____

_____

_____

You're Grateful For: _____

Your Happiest Moment Was: _____

_____

_____

How Do You Want To Be Remembered? _____

_____

_____

AUGUST 26, 20____

About Today: _____

_____

_____

_____

You're Grateful For: _____

Your Happiest Moment Was: _____

_____

_____

How Do You Want To Be Remembered? _____

_____

_____

AUGUST 27, 20___

About Today: _____

_____

_____

_____

You're Grateful For:_____

Your Happiest Moment Was: _____

_____

_____

What Are Your Most Frequent Sabotaging Thoughts? Are They True?

_____

_____

AUGUST 27, 20___

About Today: _____

_____

_____

_____

You're Grateful For:_____

Your Happiest Moment Was: _____

_____

_____

What Are Your Most Frequent Sabotaging Thoughts? Are They True?

_____

_____

AUGUST 28, 20____

About Today: _____

_____

_____

_____

You're Grateful For: _____

Your Happiest Moment Was: _____

_____

_____

What Were You Doing The Last Time You Lost Track Of Time? _____

_____

_____

AUGUST 28, 20____

About Today: _____

_____

_____

_____

You're Grateful For: _____

Your Happiest Moment Was: _____

_____

_____

What Were You Doing The Last Time You Lost Track Of Time? _____

_____

_____

AUGUST 29, 20____

About Today: _____

_____

_____

_____

You're Grateful For: _____

Your Happiest Moment Was: _____

_____

_____

When Did You Last Dance? _____

_____

_____

AUGUST 29, 20____

About Today: _____

_____

_____

_____

You're Grateful For: _____

Your Happiest Moment Was: _____

_____

_____

When Did You Last Dance? _____

_____

_____

AUGUST 30, 20____

About Today: _____

_____

_____

_____

You're Grateful For: _____

Your Happiest Moment Was: _____

_____

_____

Another Month Has Gone. How Have You Grown This Month? _____

_____

_____

AUGUST 30, 20____

About Today: _____

_____

_____

_____

You're Grateful For: _____

Your Happiest Moment Was: _____

_____

_____

Another Month Has Gone. How Have You Grown This Month? _____

_____

_____

AUGUST 31, 20____

About Today: _____

_____

_____

_____

You're Grateful For: _____

Your Happiest Moment Was: _____

_____

_____

What Do You Want To Accomplish By The End Of September? _____

_____

_____

AUGUST 31, 20____

About Today: _____

_____

_____

_____

You're Grateful For: _____

Your Happiest Moment Was: _____

_____

_____

What Do You Want To Accomplish By The End Of September? _____

_____

_____

Do Something Today

that your future self

will THANK YOU for

SEPTEMBER 1, 20____

About Today: _____

_____

_____

_____

You're Grateful For: _____

Your Happiest Moment Was: _____

_____

_____

What Do You Do To Reduce Your Impact On The Environment? _____

_____

_____

SEPTEMBER 1, 20____

About Today: _____

_____

_____

_____

You're Grateful For: _____

Your Happiest Moment Was: _____

_____

_____

What Do You Do To Reduce Your Impact On The Environment? _____

_____

_____

SEPTEMBER 2, 20___

About Today: _____

_____

_____

_____

You're Grateful For: _____

Your Happiest Moment Was: _____

_____

_____

What Would You Change, If Anything, About The Way You Were Raised?

_____

_____

SEPTEMBER 2, 20___

About Today: _____

_____

_____

_____

You're Grateful For: _____

Your Happiest Moment Was: _____

_____

_____

What Would You Change, If Anything, About The Way You Were Raised?

_____

_____

SEPTEMBER 3, 20____

About Today: _____

_____

_____

_____

You're Grateful For: _____

Your Happiest Moment Was: _____

_____

_____

What's The Most Recent Thing You Regret Spending Money On? _____

_____

_____

SEPTEMBER 3, 20____

About Today: _____

_____

_____

_____

You're Grateful For: _____

Your Happiest Moment Was: _____

_____

_____

What's The Most Recent Thing You Regret Spending Money On? _____

_____

_____

SEPTEMBER 4, 20____

About Today: _____

_____

_____

_____

You're Grateful For:_____

Your Happiest Moment Was: _____

_____

_____

Do The People Closest To You Encourage You Or Hold You Back?_____

_____

_____

SEPTEMBER 4, 20____

About Today: _____

_____

_____

_____

You're Grateful For:_____

Your Happiest Moment Was: _____

_____

_____

Do The People Closest To You Encourage You Or Hold You Back?_____

_____

_____

SEPTEMBER 5, 20____

About Today: _____

_____

_____

_____

You're Grateful For: _____

Your Happiest Moment Was: _____

_____

_____

When Was The Last Time You Cried? Why?_____

_____

_____

SEPTEMBER 5, 20____

About Today: _____

_____

_____

_____

You're Grateful For:_____

Your Happiest Moment Was: _____

_____

_____

When Was The Last Time You Cried? Why?_____

_____

_____

SEPTEMBER 6, 20___

About Today: _____

_____

_____

_____

You're Grateful For:_____

Your Happiest Moment Was: _____

_____

_____

Did You Tell Anyone You Love Them Today? Who?_____

_____

_____

SEPTEMBER 6, 20___

About Today: _____

_____

_____

_____

You're Grateful For:_____

Your Happiest Moment Was: _____

_____

_____

Did You Tell Anyone You Love Them Today? Who?_____

_____

_____

SEPTEMBER 7, 20____

About Today: _____

_____

_____

_____

You're Grateful For: _____

Your Happiest Moment Was: _____

_____

_____

What Will You Never Give Up On? _____

_____

_____

SEPTEMBER 7, 20____

About Today: _____

_____

_____

_____

You're Grateful For: _____

Your Happiest Moment Was: _____

_____

_____

What Will You Never Give Up On? _____

_____

_____

SEPTEMBER 8, 20____

About Today: _____

_____

_____

_____

You're Grateful For: _____

Your Happiest Moment Was: _____

_____

_____

If You Could Live In Any U.S. State, Which Would You Choose? Why?

_____

_____

SEPTEMBER 8, 20____

About Today: _____

_____

_____

_____

You're Grateful For:_____

Your Happiest Moment Was: _____

_____

_____

If You Could Live In Any U.S. State, Which Would You Choose? Why?

_____

_____

SEPTEMBER 9, 20____

About Today: _____

_____

_____

_____

You're Grateful For: _____

Your Happiest Moment Was: _____

_____

_____

What's The Last Thing You Broke? _____

_____

_____

SEPTEMBER 9, 20____

About Today: _____

_____

_____

_____

You're Grateful For: _____

Your Happiest Moment Was: _____

_____

_____

What's The Last Thing You Broke? _____

_____

_____

SEPTEMBER 10, 20____

About Today: _____

_____

_____

_____

You're Grateful For: _____

Your Happiest Moment Was: _____

_____

_____

Name The People You Love Most: _____

_____

_____

SEPTEMBER 10, 20____

About Today: _____

_____

_____

_____

You're Grateful For: _____

Your Happiest Moment Was: _____

_____

_____

Name The People You Love Most: _____

_____

_____

SEPTEMBER 11, 20____

About Today: _____

_____

_____

_____

You're Grateful For: _____

Your Happiest Moment Was: _____

_____

_____

Would You Rather Be Liked Or Respected? _____

_____

_____

SEPTEMBER 11, 20____

About Today: _____

_____

_____

_____

You're Grateful For: _____

Your Happiest Moment Was: _____

_____

_____

Would You Rather Be Liked Or Respected? _____

_____

_____

SEPTEMBER 12, 20____

About Today: _____

_____

_____

_____

You're Grateful For: _____

Your Happiest Moment Was: _____

_____

_____

Do You Work To Live Or Live To Work? _____

_____

_____

SEPTEMBER 12, 20____

About Today: _____

_____

_____

_____

You're Grateful For: _____

Your Happiest Moment Was: _____

_____

_____

Do You Work To Live Or Live To Work? _____

_____

_____

SEPTEMBER 13, 20____

About Today: _____

_____

_____

_____

You're Grateful For: _____

Your Happiest Moment Was: _____

_____

_____

What Do You Want To Have Achieved Three Years From Now? _____

_____

_____

SEPTEMBER 13, 20____

About Today: _____

_____

_____

_____

You're Grateful For: _____

Your Happiest Moment Was: _____

_____

_____

What Do You Want To Have Achieved Three Years From Now? _____

_____

_____

SEPTEMBER 14, 20____

About Today: _____

_____

_____

_____

You're Grateful For: _____

Your Happiest Moment Was: _____

_____

_____

Do You Give Your Loved Ones The Love & Attention They Deserve? _____

_____

_____

SEPTEMBER 14, 20____

About Today: _____

_____

_____

_____

You're Grateful For: _____

Your Happiest Moment Was: _____

_____

_____

Do You Give Your Loved Ones The Love & Attention They Deserve? _____

_____

_____

SEPTEMBER 15, 20____

About Today: _____

_____

_____

_____

You're Grateful For:_____

Your Happiest Moment Was:_____

_____

_____

What Are You Currently Reading? _____

_____

_____

SEPTEMBER 15, 20____

About Today: _____

_____

_____

_____

You're Grateful For:_____

Your Happiest Moment Was:_____

_____

_____

What Are You Currently Reading? _____

_____

_____

SEPTEMBER 16, 20____

About Today: _____

_____

_____

_____

You're Grateful For:_____

Your Happiest Moment Was: _____

_____

_____

What's Your Favorite Type Of Intimacy (Emotional, Sexual, Intellectual, etc.)?

_____

_____

SEPTEMBER 16, 20____

About Today: _____

_____

_____

_____

You're Grateful For:_____

Your Happiest Moment Was: _____

_____

_____

What's Your Favorite Type Of Intimacy (Emotional, Sexual, Intellectual, etc.)?

_____

_____

SEPTEMBER 17, 20___

About Today: _____

_____

_____

_____

You're Grateful For:_____

Your Happiest Moment Was: _____

_____

_____

If You Never Wasted Another Minute, What Might Your Life Look Like?

_____

_____

SEPTEMBER 17, 20___

About Today: _____

_____

_____

_____

You're Grateful For:_____

Your Happiest Moment Was: _____

_____

_____

If You Never Wasted Another Minute, What Might Your Life Look Like?

_____

_____

SEPTEMBER 18, 20____

About Today: _____

_____

_____

_____

You're Grateful For: _____

Your Happiest Moment Was: _____

_____

_____

Are You Obligated To Keep Things People Give You? _____

_____

_____

SEPTEMBER 18, 20____

About Today: _____

_____

_____

_____

You're Grateful For: _____

Your Happiest Moment Was: _____

_____

_____

Are You Obligated To Keep Things People Give You? _____

_____

_____

SEPTEMBER 19, 20____

About Today: _____

_____

_____

_____

You're Grateful For:_____

Your Happiest Moment Was: _____

_____

_____

What's Your Favorite Season? Why?_____

_____

_____

SEPTEMBER 19, 20____

About Today: _____

_____

_____

_____

You're Grateful For:_____

Your Happiest Moment Was: _____

_____

_____

What's Your Favorite Season? Why?_____

_____

_____

SEPTEMBER 20, 20____

About Today: _____

_____

_____

_____

You're Grateful For: _____

Your Happiest Moment Was: _____

_____

_____

What's Your Top Priority Right Now? _____

_____

_____

SEPTEMBER 20, 20____

About Today: _____

_____

_____

_____

You're Grateful For: _____

Your Happiest Moment Was: _____

_____

_____

What's Your Top Priority Right Now? _____

_____

_____

SEPTEMBER 21, 20____

About Today: _____

_____

_____

_____

You're Grateful For: _____

Your Happiest Moment Was: _____

_____

_____

Do You Fear Rejection? If So, Why? _____

_____

_____

SEPTEMBER 21, 20____

About Today: _____

_____

_____

_____

You're Grateful For: _____

Your Happiest Moment Was: _____

_____

_____

Do You Fear Rejection? If So, Why? _____

_____

_____

SEPTEMBER 22, 20____

About Today: _____

_____

_____

_____

You're Grateful For: _____

Your Happiest Moment Was: _____

_____

_____

If You Could Be Anywhere Else Right Now, Where Would You Be? _____

_____

_____

SEPTEMBER 22, 20____

About Today: _____

_____

_____

_____

You're Grateful For: _____

Your Happiest Moment Was: _____

_____

_____

If You Could Be Anywhere Else Right Now, Where Would You Be? _____

_____

_____

SEPTEMBER 23, 20____

About Today: _____

_____

_____

_____

You're Grateful For: _____

Your Happiest Moment Was: _____

_____

_____

What Do You Bring To Your Friendships? _____

_____

_____

SEPTEMBER 23, 20____

About Today: _____

_____

_____

_____

You're Grateful For: _____

Your Happiest Moment Was: _____

_____

_____

What Do You Bring To Your Friendships? _____

_____

_____

SEPTEMBER 24, 20____

About Today: _____

_____

_____

_____

You're Grateful For: _____

Your Happiest Moment Was: _____

_____

_____

Does Anyone Try To Make You Feel That You Owe Them? Do You? _____

_____

_____

SEPTEMBER 24, 20____

About Today: _____

_____

_____

_____

You're Grateful For: _____

Your Happiest Moment Was: _____

_____

_____

Does Anyone Try To Make You Feel That You Owe Them? Do You? _____

_____

_____

SEPTEMBER 25, 20____

About Today: _____

_____

_____

_____

You're Grateful For: _____

Your Happiest Moment Was: _____

_____

_____

Do You Know What You're Eating Tomorrow? _____

_____

_____

SEPTEMBER 25, 20____

About Today: _____

_____

_____

_____

You're Grateful For: _____

Your Happiest Moment Was: _____

_____

_____

Do You Know What You're Eating Tomorrow? _____

_____

_____

SEPTEMBER 26, 20____

About Today: _____

_____

_____

_____

You're Grateful For: _____

Your Happiest Moment Was: _____

_____

_____

How Can You Achieve Your Ideal Diet? _____

_____

_____

SEPTEMBER 26, 20____

About Today: _____

_____

_____

_____

You're Grateful For: _____

Your Happiest Moment Was: _____

_____

_____

How Can You Achieve Your Ideal Diet? _____

_____

_____

SEPTEMBER 27, 20___

About Today: _____

_____

_____

_____

You're Grateful For: _____

Your Happiest Moment Was: _____

_____

_____

What Are Your Favorite Sounds? _____

_____

_____

SEPTEMBER 27, 20___

About Today: _____

_____

_____

_____

You're Grateful For: _____

Your Happiest Moment Was: _____

_____

_____

What Are Your Favorite Sounds? _____

_____

_____

SEPTEMBER 28, 20____

About Today: _____

_____

_____

_____

You're Grateful For: _____

Your Happiest Moment Was: _____

_____

_____

What Limiting Beliefs Might You Be Holding On To? _____

_____

_____

SEPTEMBER 28, 20____

About Today: _____

_____

_____

_____

You're Grateful For: _____

Your Happiest Moment Was: _____

_____

_____

What Limiting Beliefs Might You Be Holding On To? _____

_____

_____

SEPTEMBER 29, 20____

About Today: _____

_____

_____

_____

You're Grateful For: _____

Your Happiest Moment Was: _____

_____

_____

Another Month Has Gone. What Changed This Month? _____

_____

_____

SEPTEMBER 29, 20____

About Today: _____

_____

_____

_____

You're Grateful For: _____

Your Happiest Moment Was: _____

_____

_____

Another Month Has Gone. What Changed This Month? _____

_____

_____

SEPTEMBER 30, 20____

About Today: _____

_____

_____

_____

You're Grateful For: _____

Your Happiest Moment Was: _____

_____

_____

What Do You Want To Accomplish By The End Of October? _____

_____

_____

SEPTEMBER 30, 20____

About Today: _____

_____

_____

_____

You're Grateful For: _____

Your Happiest Moment Was: _____

_____

_____

What Do You Want To Accomplish By The End Of October? _____

_____

_____

THE BEST WAY TO PREDICT
YOUR FUTURE IS TO
CREATE IT

-Alan Kay

OCTOBER 1, 20____

About Today: _____

_____

_____

_____

You're Grateful For: _____

Your Happiest Moment Was: _____

_____

_____

What's Your Ideal Home Like? _____

_____

_____

OCTOBER 1, 20____

About Today: _____

_____

_____

_____

You're Grateful For: _____

Your Happiest Moment Was: _____

_____

_____

What's Your Ideal Home Like? _____

_____

_____

OCTOBER 2, 20___

About Today: _____

_____

_____

_____

You're Grateful For: _____

Your Happiest Moment Was: _____

_____

_____

Do You Include Yourself Among Those You Love Most? If No, Why Not?

_____

_____

OCTOBER 2, 20___

About Today: _____

_____

_____

_____

You're Grateful For: _____

Your Happiest Moment Was: _____

_____

_____

Do You Include Yourself Among Those You Love Most? If No, Why Not?

_____

_____

OCTOBER 3, 20____

About Today: _____

_____

_____

_____

You're Grateful For: _____

Your Happiest Moment Was: _____

_____

_____

How Might You Be Prioritizing Money Over Relationships? _____

_____

_____

OCTOBER 3, 20____

About Today: _____

_____

_____

_____

You're Grateful For: _____

Your Happiest Moment Was: _____

_____

_____

How Might You Be Prioritizing Money Over Relationships? _____

_____

_____

OCTOBER 4, 20____

About Today: _____

_____

_____

_____

You're Grateful For: _____

Your Happiest Moment Was: _____

_____

_____

Who Is Your Very Best Friend & What Do You Love Most About Him/Her?

_____

_____

OCTOBER 4, 20____

About Today: _____

_____

_____

_____

You're Grateful For: _____

Your Happiest Moment Was: _____

_____

_____

Who Is Your Very Best Friend & What Do You Love Most About Him/Her?

_____

_____

OCTOBER 5, 20____

About Today: _____

_____

_____

_____

You're Grateful For: _____

Your Happiest Moment Was: _____

_____

_____

Did Anything Surprise You Today? _____

_____

_____

OCTOBER 5, 20____

About Today: _____

_____

_____

_____

You're Grateful For: _____

Your Happiest Moment Was: _____

_____

_____

Did Anything Surprise You Today? _____

_____

_____

OCTOBER 6, 20____

About Today: _____

_____

_____

_____

You're Grateful For: _____

Your Happiest Moment Was: _____

_____

_____

Which Part Of Your Body Do You Admire Most? _____

_____

_____

OCTOBER 6, 20____

About Today: _____

_____

_____

_____

You're Grateful For: _____

Your Happiest Moment Was: _____

_____

_____

Which Part Of Your Body Do You Admire Most? _____

_____

_____

OCTOBER 7, 20____

About Today: _____

_____

_____

_____

You're Grateful For: _____

Your Happiest Moment Was: _____

_____

_____

How Can You Achieve Your Ideal Home? _____

_____

_____

OCTOBER 7, 20____

About Today: _____

_____

_____

_____

You're Grateful For: _____

Your Happiest Moment Was: _____

_____

_____

How Can You Achieve Your Ideal Home? _____

_____

_____

OCTOBER 8, 20___

About Today: _____

_____

_____

_____

You're Grateful For: _____

Your Happiest Moment Was: _____

_____

_____

What's Your Favorite Way To Spend A Rainy Sunday Morning? _____

_____

_____

OCTOBER 8, 20___

About Today: _____

_____

_____

_____

You're Grateful For: _____

Your Happiest Moment Was: _____

_____

_____

What's Your Favorite Way To Spend A Rainy Sunday Morning? _____

_____

_____

OCTOBER 9, 20___

About Today: _____

_____

_____

_____

You're Grateful For: _____

Your Happiest Moment Was: _____

_____

_____

What's One Of Your Fondest Teenage Memories? ____

_____

_____

OCTOBER 9, 20___

About Today: _____

_____

_____

_____

You're Grateful For: _____

Your Happiest Moment Was: _____

_____

_____

What's One Of Your Fondest Teenage Memories? ____

_____

_____

OCTOBER 10, 20____

About Today: _____

_____

_____

_____

You're Grateful For: _____

Your Happiest Moment Was: _____

_____

_____

What Are You Passionate About? _____

_____

_____

OCTOBER 10, 20____

About Today: _____

_____

_____

_____

You're Grateful For: _____

Your Happiest Moment Was: _____

_____

_____

What Are You Passionate About? _____

_____

_____

OCTOBER 11, 20____

About Today: _____

_____

_____

_____

You're Grateful For:_____

Your Happiest Moment Was: _____

_____

_____

When Was The Last Time You Pushed Yourself To Your Physical Limits?

_____

_____

OCTOBER 11, 20____

About Today: _____

_____

_____

_____

You're Grateful For:_____

Your Happiest Moment Was: _____

_____

_____

When Was The Last Time You Pushed Yourself To Your Physical Limits?

_____

_____

OCTOBER 12, 20____

About Today: _____

_____

_____

_____

You're Grateful For: _____

Your Happiest Moment Was: _____

_____

_____

What Makes You Feel Anxious? _____

_____

_____

OCTOBER 12, 20____

About Today: _____

_____

_____

_____

You're Grateful For: _____

Your Happiest Moment Was: _____

_____

_____

What Makes You Feel Anxious? _____

_____

_____

OCTOBER 13, 20____

About Today: _____

_____

_____

_____

You're Grateful For: _____

Your Happiest Moment Was: _____

_____

_____

If Not Now, When? _____

_____

_____

OCTOBER 13, 20____

About Today: _____

_____

_____

_____

You're Grateful For: _____

Your Happiest Moment Was: _____

_____

_____

If Not Now, When? _____

_____

_____

OCTOBER 14, 20____

About Today: _____

_____

_____

_____

You're Grateful For: _____

Your Happiest Moment Was: _____

_____

_____

What Kind Of Person Do You Most Enjoy Spending Time With? _____

_____

_____

OCTOBER 14, 20____

About Today: _____

_____

_____

_____

You're Grateful For: _____

Your Happiest Moment Was: _____

_____

_____

What Kind Of Person Do You Most Enjoy Spending Time With? _____

_____

_____

OCTOBER 15, 20____

About Today: _____

_____

_____

_____

You're Grateful For: _____

Your Happiest Moment Was: _____

_____

_____

What Stressed You Today? Will It Matter In 5 Weeks? 5 Days? Tomorrow?

_____

_____

OCTOBER 15, 20____

About Today: _____

_____

_____

_____

You're Grateful For: _____

Your Happiest Moment Was: _____

_____

_____

What Stressed You Today? Will It Matter In 5 Weeks? 5 Days? Tomorrow?

_____

_____

OCTOBER 16, 20____

About Today: _____

_____

_____

_____

You're Grateful For:_____

Your Happiest Moment Was: _____

_____

_____

What's Your Favorite Comfort Food? Describe The Way It Makes You Feel.

_____

_____

OCTOBER 16, 20____

About Today: _____

_____

_____

_____

You're Grateful For:_____

Your Happiest Moment Was: _____

_____

_____

What's Your Favorite Comfort Food? Describe The Way It Makes You Feel.

_____

_____

OCTOBER 17, 20____

About Today: _____

_____

_____

_____

You're Grateful For: _____

Your Happiest Moment Was: _____

_____

_____

When Did You Last Have An Exciting Idea? Are You Pursuing That Idea?

_____

_____

OCTOBER 17, 20____

About Today: _____

_____

_____

_____

You're Grateful For: _____

Your Happiest Moment Was: _____

_____

_____

When Did You Last Have An Exciting Idea? Are You Pursuing That Idea?

_____

_____

OCTOBER 18, 20____

About Today: _____

_____

_____

_____

You're Grateful For: _____

Your Happiest Moment Was: _____

_____

_____

How Much Money Is Enough? _____

_____

_____

OCTOBER 18, 20____

About Today: _____

_____

_____

_____

You're Grateful For: _____

Your Happiest Moment Was: _____

_____

_____

How Much Money Is Enough? _____

_____

_____

OCTOBER 19, 20____

About Today: _____

_____

_____

_____

You're Grateful For: _____

Your Happiest Moment Was: _____

_____

_____

What Do You Want To Have Achieved Ten Years From Now? _____

_____

_____

OCTOBER 19, 20____

About Today: _____

_____

_____

_____

You're Grateful For: _____

Your Happiest Moment Was: _____

_____

_____

What Do You Want To Have Achieved Ten Years From Now? _____

_____

_____

OCTOBER 20, 20___

About Today: _____

_____

_____

_____

You're Grateful For: _____

Your Happiest Moment Was: _____

_____

_____

Do You Mind Your Own Business Or Meddle In The Business Of Others?

_____

_____

OCTOBER 20, 20___

About Today: _____

_____

_____

_____

You're Grateful For: _____

Your Happiest Moment Was: _____

_____

_____

Do You Mind Your Own Business Or Meddle In The Business Of Others?

_____

_____

OCTOBER 21, 20____

About Today: _____

_____

_____

_____

You're Grateful For: _____

Your Happiest Moment Was: _____

_____

_____

Do You Ask For What You Need? _____

_____

_____

OCTOBER 21, 20____

About Today: _____

_____

_____

_____

You're Grateful For: _____

Your Happiest Moment Was: _____

_____

_____

Do You Ask For What You Need? _____

_____

_____

OCTOBER 22, 20____

About Today: _____

_____

_____

_____

You're Grateful For:_____

Your Happiest Moment Was: _____

_____

_____

In What Ways Do You Procrastinate? _____

_____

_____

OCTOBER 22, 20____

About Today: _____

_____

_____

_____

You're Grateful For:_____

Your Happiest Moment Was: _____

_____

_____

In What Ways Do You Procrastinate? _____

_____

_____

OCTOBER 23, 20____

About Today: _____

_____

_____

_____

You're Grateful For: _____

Your Happiest Moment Was: _____

_____

_____

How Would You Spend One Million Dollars? _____

_____

_____

OCTOBER 23, 20____

About Today: _____

_____

_____

_____

You're Grateful For: _____

Your Happiest Moment Was: _____

_____

_____

How Would You Spend One Million Dollars? _____

_____

_____

OCTOBER 24, 20____

About Today: _____

_____

_____

_____

You're Grateful For: _____

Your Happiest Moment Was: _____

_____

_____

How Can You Be A Better Daughter/Son? _____

_____

_____

OCTOBER 24, 20____

About Today: _____

_____

_____

_____

You're Grateful For: _____

Your Happiest Moment Was: _____

_____

_____

How Can You Be A Better Daughter/Son? _____

_____

_____

OCTOBER 25, 20____

About Today: _____

_____

_____

_____

You're Grateful For:_____

Your Happiest Moment Was: _____

_____

_____

What's One Of The Nicest Things You've Ever Done For Someone?_____

_____

_____

OCTOBER 25, 20____

About Today: _____

_____

_____

_____

You're Grateful For:_____

Your Happiest Moment Was: _____

_____

_____

What's One Of The Nicest Things You've Ever Done For Someone?_____

_____

_____

OCTOBER 26, 20____

About Today: _____

_____

_____

_____

You're Grateful For: _____

Your Happiest Moment Was: _____

_____

_____

What Did You Love Doing As A Child? Do You Still Do Anything Like It?

_____

_____

OCTOBER 26, 20____

About Today: _____

_____

_____

_____

You're Grateful For: _____

Your Happiest Moment Was: _____

_____

_____

What Did You Love Doing As A Child? Do You Still Do Anything Like It?

_____

_____

OCTOBER 27, 20____

About Today: _____

_____

_____

_____

You're Grateful For: _____

Your Happiest Moment Was: _____

_____

_____

How Can You Make Your Life More Meaningful, Starting Today? _____

_____

_____

OCTOBER 27, 20____

About Today: _____

_____

_____

_____

You're Grateful For: _____

Your Happiest Moment Was: _____

_____

How Can You Make Your Life More Meaningful, Starting Today? _____

_____

_____

OCTOBER 28, 20____

About Today: _____

_____

_____

_____

You're Grateful For: _____

Your Happiest Moment Was: _____

_____

_____

What's Your Ideal Weight? _____

_____

_____

OCTOBER 28, 20____

About Today: _____

_____

_____

_____

You're Grateful For: _____

Your Happiest Moment Was: _____

_____

_____

What's Your Ideal Weight? _____

_____

_____

OCTOBER 29, 20____

About Today: _____

_____

_____

_____

You're Grateful For: _____

Your Happiest Moment Was: _____

_____

_____

When Was The Last Time You Went Somewhere New? _____

_____

_____

OCTOBER 29, 20____

About Today: _____

_____

_____

_____

You're Grateful For: _____

Your Happiest Moment Was: _____

_____

_____

When Was The Last Time You Went Somewhere New? _____

_____

_____

OCTOBER 30, 20____

About Today: _____

_____

_____

_____

You're Grateful For: _____

Your Happiest Moment Was: _____

_____

_____

Another Month Has Gone. What's Your Favorite Memory from October?

_____

_____

OCTOBER 30, 20____

About Today: _____

_____

_____

_____

You're Grateful For: _____

Your Happiest Moment Was: _____

_____

_____

Another Month Has Gone. What's Your Favorite Memory from October?

_____

_____

OCTOBER 31, 20____

About Today: _____

_____

_____

_____

You're Grateful For: _____

Your Happiest Moment Was: _____

_____

_____

What Do You Want To Accomplish By The End Of November? _____

_____

_____

OCTOBER 31, 20____

About Today: _____

_____

_____

_____

You're Grateful For: _____

Your Happiest Moment Was: _____

_____

_____

What Do You Want To Accomplish By The End Of November? _____

_____

_____

If It Doesn't Add
To Your Life,
It Doesn't Belong
In Your Life.

NOVEMBER 1, 20____

About Today: _____

_____

_____

_____

You're Grateful For: _____

Your Happiest Moment Was: _____

_____

_____

What's Your Idea Of A Perfect Date? _____

_____

_____

NOVEMBER 1, 20____

About Today: _____

_____

_____

_____

You're Grateful For: _____

Your Happiest Moment Was: _____

_____

_____

What's Your Idea Of A Perfect Date? _____

_____

_____

NOVEMBER 2, 20___

About Today: _____

_____

_____

_____

You're Grateful For: _____

Your Happiest Moment Was: _____

_____

_____

How Do You Know When It's Time To Let Go Of Something Or Someone?

_____

_____

NOVEMBER 2, 20___

About Today: _____

_____

_____

_____

You're Grateful For: _____

Your Happiest Moment Was: _____

_____

_____

How Do You Know When It's Time To Let Go Of Something Or Someone?

_____

_____

NOVEMBER 3, 20____

About Today: _____

_____

_____

_____

You're Grateful For: _____

Your Happiest Moment Was: _____

_____

_____

How Can You Be A Better Brother/Sister? _____

_____

NOVEMBER 3, 20____

About Today: _____

_____

_____

You're Grateful For: _____

Your Happiest Moment Was: _____

_____

How Can You Be A Better Brother/Sister? _____

_____

_____

NOVEMBER 4, 20___

About Today: _____

_____

_____

_____

You're Grateful For: _____

Your Happiest Moment Was: _____

_____

_____

How Can You Achieve Your Ideal Weight? _____

_____

_____

NOVEMBER 4, 20___

About Today: _____

_____

_____

_____

You're Grateful For: _____

Your Happiest Moment Was: _____

_____

_____

How Can You Achieve Your Ideal Weight? _____

_____

_____

NOVEMBER 5, 20____

About Today: _____

_____

_____

_____

You're Grateful For: _____

Your Happiest Moment Was: _____

_____

_____

What's The Most Beautiful Thing You've Ever Seen? _____

_____

NOVEMBER 5, 20____

About Today: _____

_____

_____

_____

You're Grateful For: _____

Your Happiest Moment Was: _____

_____

_____

What's The Most Beautiful Thing You've Ever Seen? _____

_____

NOVEMBER 6, 20____

About Today: _____

_____

_____

_____

You're Grateful For: _____

Your Happiest Moment Was: _____

_____

_____

What Can You Do To Benefit Humanity Every Day? _____

_____

_____

NOVEMBER 6, 20____

About Today: _____

_____

_____

_____

You're Grateful For: _____

Your Happiest Moment Was: _____

_____

_____

What Can You Do To Benefit Humanity Every Day? _____

_____

_____

NOVEMBER 7, 20___

About Today: _____

_____

_____

_____

You're Grateful For: _____

Your Happiest Moment Was: _____

_____

_____

Do You Apologize Unnecessarily? Why? _____

_____

_____

NOVEMBER 7, 20___

About Today: _____

_____

_____

_____

You're Grateful For: _____

Your Happiest Moment Was: _____

_____

_____

Do You Apologize Unnecessarily? Why? _____

_____

_____

NOVEMBER 8, 20____

About Today: _____

_____

_____

_____

You're Grateful For: _____

Your Happiest Moment Was: _____

_____

_____

If You Could Ask Your Future-Self One Question, What Would You Ask?

_____

_____

NOVEMBER 8, 20____

About Today: _____

_____

_____

_____

You're Grateful For: _____

Your Happiest Moment Was: _____

_____

_____

If You Could Ask Your Future-Self One Question, What Would You Ask?

_____

_____

NOVEMBER 9, 20____

About Today: _____

_____

_____

_____

You're Grateful For:_____

Your Happiest Moment Was: _____

_____

_____

What's Your Dream Job?_____

_____

_____

NOVEMBER 9, 20____

About Today: _____

_____

_____

_____

You're Grateful For:_____

Your Happiest Moment Was: _____

_____

_____

What's Your Dream Job?_____

_____

_____

NOVEMBER 10, 20___

About Today: _____

_____

_____

_____

You're Grateful For: _____

Your Happiest Moment Was: _____

_____

_____

If You Could Instill Something In A Newborn Baby's Mind, What Would It Be?

_____

_____

NOVEMBER 10, 20___

About Today: _____

_____

_____

_____

You're Grateful For: _____

Your Happiest Moment Was: _____

_____

_____

If You Could Instill Something In A Newborn Baby's Mind, What Would It Be?

_____

_____

NOVEMBER 11, 20____

About Today: _____

_____

_____

_____

You're Grateful For: _____

Your Happiest Moment Was: _____

_____

_____

What Are You Doing When You Feel Most Beautiful? _____

_____

_____

NOVEMBER 11, 20____

About Today: _____

_____

_____

_____

You're Grateful For: _____

Your Happiest Moment Was: _____

_____

_____

What Are You Doing When You Feel Most Beautiful? _____

_____

_____

NOVEMBER 12, 20____

About Today: _____

_____

_____

_____

You're Grateful For: _____

Your Happiest Moment Was: _____

_____

_____

What Can You Learn From Those Who Have Achieved Similar Goals To Yours?

_____

_____

NOVEMBER 12, 20____

About Today: _____

_____

_____

_____

You're Grateful For: _____

Your Happiest Moment Was: _____

_____

_____

What Can You Learn From Those Who Have Achieved Similar Goals To Yours?

_____

_____

NOVEMBER 13, 20____

About Today: _____

_____

_____

_____

You're Grateful For: _____

Your Happiest Moment Was: _____

_____

_____

What Are/Were Your Parent's Best Qualities? _____

_____

_____

NOVEMBER 13, 20____

About Today: _____

_____

_____

_____

You're Grateful For: _____

Your Happiest Moment Was: _____

_____

_____

What Are/Were Your Parent's Best Qualities? _____

_____

_____

NOVEMBER 14, 20___

About Today: _____

_____

_____

_____

You're Grateful For: _____

Your Happiest Moment Was: _____

_____

_____

Do You Feel Your Childhood Was Better Or Worse Than Most Others?

_____

_____

NOVEMBER 14, 20___

About Today: _____

_____

_____

_____

You're Grateful For: _____

Your Happiest Moment Was: _____

_____

_____

Do You Feel Your Childhood Was Better Or Worse Than Most Others?

_____

_____

NOVEMBER 15, 20____

About Today: _____

_____

_____

_____

You're Grateful For: _____

Your Happiest Moment Was: _____

_____

_____

Have You Ever Invested In Yourself Financially? _____

_____

_____

NOVEMBER 15, 20____

About Today: _____

_____

_____

_____

You're Grateful For: _____

Your Happiest Moment Was: _____

_____

_____

Have You Ever Invested In Yourself Financially? _____

_____

_____

NOVEMBER 16, 20___

About Today: _____

_____

_____

_____

You're Grateful For: _____

Your Happiest Moment Was: _____

_____

_____

Did You Pass Up An Opportunity To Be Kind Or Generous Today? If So, Why?

_____

_____

NOVEMBER 16, 20___

About Today: _____

_____

_____

_____

You're Grateful For: _____

Your Happiest Moment Was: _____

_____

_____

Did You Pass Up An Opportunity To Be Kind Or Generous Today? If So, Why?

_____

_____

NOVEMBER 17, 20____

About Today: _____

_____

_____

_____

You're Grateful For: _____

Your Happiest Moment Was: _____

_____

_____

How Can You Love Yourself More Today? _____

_____

_____

NOVEMBER 17, 20____

About Today: _____

_____

_____

_____

You're Grateful For: _____

Your Happiest Moment Was: _____

_____

_____

How Can You Love Yourself More Today? _____

_____

_____

NOVEMBER 18, 20____

About Today: _____

_____

_____

_____

You're Grateful For: _____

Your Happiest Moment Was: _____

_____

_____

What's The Most Important Thing You Can Do Right Now? _____

_____

_____

NOVEMBER 18, 20____

About Today: _____

_____

_____

_____

You're Grateful For: _____

Your Happiest Moment Was: _____

_____

_____

What's The Most Important Thing You Can Do Right Now? _____

_____

_____

NOVEMBER 19, 20____

About Today: _____

_____

_____

_____

You're Grateful For: _____

Your Happiest Moment Was: _____

_____

_____

How Do You Manage Stress? Can You Manage It Better? _____

_____

_____

NOVEMBER 19, 20____

About Today: _____

_____

_____

_____

You're Grateful For: _____

Your Happiest Moment Was: _____

_____

_____

How Do You Manage Stress? Can You Manage It Better? _____

_____

_____

NOVEMBER 20, 20___

About Today: _____

_____

_____

_____

You're Grateful For:_____

Your Happiest Moment Was: _____

_____

_____

What Question Do You Need Someone To Ask You?_____

_____

_____

NOVEMBER 20, 20___

About Today: _____

_____

_____

_____

You're Grateful For:_____

Your Happiest Moment Was: _____

_____

_____

What Question Do You Need Someone To Ask You?_____

_____

_____

NOVEMBER 21, 20____

About Today: _____

_____

_____

_____

You're Grateful For: _____

Your Happiest Moment Was: _____

_____

_____

Do You Allow People To Disrespect Your Boundaries? _____

_____

_____

NOVEMBER 21, 20____

About Today: _____

_____

_____

_____

You're Grateful For: _____

Your Happiest Moment Was: _____

_____

_____

Do You Allow People To Disrespect Your Boundaries? _____

_____

_____

NOVEMBER 22, 20___

About Today: _____

_____

_____

_____

You're Grateful For: _____

Your Happiest Moment Was: _____

_____

_____

What's Your Favorite Physical Activity? How Often Do You Do It? _____

_____

_____

NOVEMBER 22, 20___

About Today: _____

_____

_____

_____

You're Grateful For: _____

Your Happiest Moment Was: _____

_____

_____

What's Your Favorite Physical Activity? How Often Do You Do It? _____

_____

_____

NOVEMBER 23, 20____

About Today: _____

_____

_____

_____

You're Grateful For:_____

Your Happiest Moment Was: _____

_____

_____

What Can You Do Differently To Be More Present With Your Loved Ones?

_____

_____

NOVEMBER 23, 20____

About Today: _____

_____

_____

_____

You're Grateful For:_____

Your Happiest Moment Was: _____

_____

_____

What Can You Do Differently To Be More Present With Your Loved Ones?

_____

_____

NOVEMBER 24, 20___

About Today: _____

_____

_____

_____

You're Grateful For: _____

Your Happiest Moment Was: _____

_____

_____

When It's All Said & Done, Will You Have Said More Than You've Done?

_____

_____

NOVEMBER 24, 20___

About Today: _____

_____

_____

_____

You're Grateful For: _____

Your Happiest Moment Was: _____

_____

_____

When It's All Said & Done, Will You Have Said More Than You've Done?

_____

_____

NOVEMBER 25, 20____

About Today: _____

_____

_____

_____

You're Grateful For: _____

Your Happiest Moment Was: _____

_____

_____

How Do You Celebrate Your Achievements? _____

_____

_____

NOVEMBER 25, 20____

About Today: _____

_____

_____

_____

You're Grateful For: _____

Your Happiest Moment Was: _____

_____

_____

How Do You Celebrate Your Achievements? _____

_____

_____

NOVEMBER 26, 20___

About Today: _____

_____

_____

_____

You're Grateful For: _____

Your Happiest Moment Was: _____

_____

_____

Did You Play & Have Fun Today? _____

_____

_____

NOVEMBER 26, 20___

About Today: _____

_____

_____

_____

You're Grateful For: _____

Your Happiest Moment Was: _____

_____

_____

Did You Play & Have Fun Today? _____

_____

_____

NOVEMBER 27, 20___

About Today: _____

_____

_____

_____

You're Grateful For: _____

Your Happiest Moment Was: _____

_____

_____

What Does Your Inner Child Need? Can You Give It To Him/Her? _____

_____

_____

NOVEMBER 27, 20___

About Today: _____

_____

_____

_____

You're Grateful For: _____

Your Happiest Moment Was: _____

_____

_____

What Does Your Inner Child Need? Can You Give It To Him/Her? _____

_____

_____

NOVEMBER 28, 20____

About Today: _____

_____

_____

_____

You're Grateful For: _____

Your Happiest Moment Was: _____

_____

_____

Are You Capable Of Forgiving Someone Who Didn't Apologize?_____

_____

_____

NOVEMBER 28, 20____

About Today: _____

_____

_____

_____

You're Grateful For: _____

Your Happiest Moment Was: _____

_____

_____

Are You Capable Of Forgiving Someone Who Didn't Apologize?_____

_____

_____

NOVEMBER 29, 20____

About Today: _____

_____

_____

_____

You're Grateful For: _____

Your Happiest Moment Was: _____

_____

_____

Another Month Has Gone. What Did You Accomplish? _____

_____

_____

NOVEMBER 29, 20____

About Today: _____

_____

_____

_____

You're Grateful For: _____

Your Happiest Moment Was: _____

_____

_____

Another Month Has Gone. What Did You Accomplish? _____

_____

_____

NOVEMBER 30, 20____

About Today: _____

_____

_____

_____

You're Grateful For: _____

Your Happiest Moment Was: _____

_____

_____

What Do You Want To Accomplish By The End Of The Year? _____

_____

_____

NOVEMBER 30, 20____

About Today: _____

_____

_____

_____

You're Grateful For: _____

Your Happiest Moment Was: _____

_____

_____

What Do You Want To Accomplish By The End Of The Year? _____

_____

_____

How we spend our DAYS

is, of course,

how we spend our LIVES

-Annie Dillard

DECEMBER 1, 20____

About Today: _____

_____

_____

_____

You're Grateful For: _____

Your Happiest Moment Was: _____

_____

_____

When Did You Last Push The Boundaries Of Your Comfort Zone? _____

_____

_____

DECEMBER 1, 20____

About Today: _____

_____

_____

_____

You're Grateful For: _____

Your Happiest Moment Was: _____

_____

_____

When Did You Last Push The Boundaries Of Your Comfort Zone? _____

_____

_____

DECEMBER 2, 20____

About Today: _____

_____

_____

_____

You're Grateful For: _____

Your Happiest Moment Was: _____

_____

_____

In What Ways Are You Your Own Worst Enemy? _____

_____

_____

DECEMBER 2, 20____

About Today: _____

_____

_____

_____

You're Grateful For: _____

Your Happiest Moment Was: _____

_____

_____

In What Ways Are You Your Own Worst Enemy? _____

_____

_____

DECEMBER 3, 20____

About Today: _____

_____

_____

_____

You're Grateful For: _____

Your Happiest Moment Was: _____

_____

_____

How Can You Be A Better Partner? _____

_____

_____

DECEMBER 3, 20____

About Today: _____

_____

_____

_____

You're Grateful For: _____

Your Happiest Moment Was: _____

_____

_____

How Can You Be A Better Partner? _____

_____

_____

DECEMBER 4, 20____

About Today: _____

_____

_____

_____

You're Grateful For: _____

Your Happiest Moment Was: _____

_____

_____

If You Didn't Have To Work For One Year, What Would You Do Instead?

_____

_____

DECEMBER 4, 20____

About Today: _____

_____

_____

_____

You're Grateful For: _____

Your Happiest Moment Was: _____

_____

If You Didn't Have To Work For One Year, What Would You Do Instead?

_____

_____

DECEMBER 5, 20____

About Today: _____

_____

_____

_____

You're Grateful For: _____

Your Happiest Moment Was: _____

_____

_____

Are You Holding On To Something You Should Let Go Of? _____

_____

_____

DECEMBER 5, 20____

About Today: _____

_____

_____

_____

You're Grateful For: _____

Your Happiest Moment Was: _____

_____

_____

Are You Holding On To Something You Should Let Go Of? _____

_____

_____

DECEMBER 6, 20____

About Today: _____

_____

_____

_____

You're Grateful For: _____

Your Happiest Moment Was: _____

_____

_____

Did You Let Anyone Down Today? What About Yourself? ____

_____

_____

DECEMBER 6, 20____

About Today: _____

_____

_____

_____

You're Grateful For: _____

Your Happiest Moment Was: _____

_____

_____

Did You Let Anyone Down Today? What About Yourself? ____

_____

_____

DECEMBER 7, 20____

About Today: _____

_____

_____

_____

You're Grateful For:_____

Your Happiest Moment Was: _____

_____

_____

Which Aspect Of Your Life Do You Want To Improve Most? _____

_____

_____

DECEMBER 7, 20____

About Today: _____

_____

_____

_____

You're Grateful For:_____

Your Happiest Moment Was: _____

_____

_____

Which Aspect Of Your Life Do You Want To Improve Most? _____

_____

_____

DECEMBER 8, 20____

About Today: _____

_____

_____

_____

You're Grateful For: _____

Your Happiest Moment Was: _____

_____

_____

What Are You Leaving Unfinished That Requires Your Attention? _____

_____

_____

DECEMBER 8, 20____

About Today: _____

_____

_____

_____

You're Grateful For: _____

Your Happiest Moment Was: _____

_____

_____

What Are You Leaving Unfinished That Requires Your Attention? _____

_____

_____

DECEMBER 9, 20____

About Today: _____

_____

_____

_____

You're Grateful For: _____

Your Happiest Moment Was: _____

_____

_____

What's Your Favorite Winter Activity? _____

_____

_____

DECEMBER 9, 20____

About Today: _____

_____

_____

_____

You're Grateful For: _____

Your Happiest Moment Was: _____

_____

_____

What's Your Favorite Winter Activity? _____

_____

_____

DECEMBER 10, 20____

About Today: _____

_____

_____

_____

You're Grateful For:_____

Your Happiest Moment Was: _____

_____

_____

Do You Pretend To Like Things That You Don't? Why? _____

_____

_____

DECEMBER 10, 20____

About Today: _____

_____

_____

_____

You're Grateful For:_____

Your Happiest Moment Was: _____

_____

Do You Pretend To Like Things That You Don't? Why? _____

_____

_____

DECEMBER 11, 20____

About Today: _____

_____

_____

_____

You're Grateful For: _____

Your Happiest Moment Was: _____

_____

_____

What Makes You *You*? _____

_____

_____

DECEMBER 11, 20____

About Today: _____

_____

_____

_____

You're Grateful For: _____

Your Happiest Moment Was: _____

_____

_____

What Makes You *You*? _____

_____

_____

DECEMBER 12, 20___

About Today: _____

_____

_____

_____

You're Grateful For:_____

Your Happiest Moment Was: _____

_____

_____

What's The Last Thing You Created? _____

_____

_____

DECEMBER 12, 20___

About Today: _____

_____

_____

_____

You're Grateful For:_____

Your Happiest Moment Was: _____

_____

_____

What's The Last Thing You Created? _____

_____

_____

DECEMBER 13, 20____

About Today: _____

_____

_____

_____

You're Grateful For: _____

Your Happiest Moment Was: _____

_____

_____

What's Your Least Favorite Holiday & Why? _____

_____

_____

DECEMBER 13, 20____

About Today: _____

_____

_____

_____

You're Grateful For: _____

Your Happiest Moment Was: _____

_____

_____

What's Your Least Favorite Holiday & Why? _____

_____

_____

DECEMBER 14, 20____

About Today: _____

_____

_____

_____

You're Grateful For: _____

Your Happiest Moment Was: _____

_____

_____

Do You Spend A Lot Of Time Doing Things You Don't Enjoy? If So, Why?

_____

_____

DECEMBER 14, 20____

About Today: _____

_____

_____

_____

You're Grateful For: _____

Your Happiest Moment Was: _____

_____

_____

Do You Spend A Lot Of Time Doing Things You Don't Enjoy? If So, Why?

_____

_____

DECEMBER 15, 20____

About Today: _____

_____

_____

_____

You're Grateful For:_____

Your Happiest Moment Was: _____

_____

_____

How Might You Be Prioritizing Material Things Over Your Values? _____

_____

_____

DECEMBER 15, 20____

About Today: _____

_____

_____

_____

You're Grateful For:_____

Your Happiest Moment Was: _____

_____

_____

How Might You Be Prioritizing Material Things Over Your Values? _____

_____

_____

DECEMBER 16, 20____

About Today: _____

_____

_____

_____

You're Grateful For: _____

Your Happiest Moment Was: _____

_____

_____

What Made You Laugh Today? _____

_____

_____

DECEMBER 16, 20____

About Today: _____

_____

_____

_____

You're Grateful For: _____

Your Happiest Moment Was: _____

_____

_____

What Made You Laugh Today? _____

_____

_____

DECEMBER 17, 20____

About Today: _____

_____

_____

_____

You're Grateful For:_____

Your Happiest Moment Was: _____

_____

_____

Do You Need A Reason To Feel Happy?_____

_____

_____

DECEMBER 17, 20____

About Today: _____

_____

_____

_____

You're Grateful For:_____

Your Happiest Moment Was: _____

_____

_____

Do You Need A Reason To Feel Happy?_____

_____

_____

DECEMBER 18, 20____

About Today: _____

_____

_____

_____

You're Grateful For: _____

Your Happiest Moment Was: _____

_____

_____

What Would You Do If You Knew No One Would Judge You? _____

_____

_____

DECEMBER 18, 20____

About Today: _____

_____

_____

_____

You're Grateful For:_____

Your Happiest Moment Was: _____

_____

_____

What Would You Do If You Knew No One Would Judge You? _____

_____

_____

DECEMBER 19, 20____

About Today: _____

_____

_____

_____

You're Grateful For: _____

Your Happiest Moment Was: _____

_____

_____

Describe Your Future In Three Words: _____

_____

_____

DECEMBER 19, 20____

About Today: _____

_____

_____

_____

You're Grateful For: _____

Your Happiest Moment Was: _____

_____

_____

Describe Your Future In Three Words: _____

_____

_____

DECEMBER 20, 20___

About Today: _____

_____

_____

_____

You're Grateful For: _____

Your Happiest Moment Was: _____

_____

_____

What Do You Want To Be When You Grow Up *More*? _____

_____

_____

DECEMBER 20, 20___

About Today: _____

_____

_____

_____

You're Grateful For: _____

Your Happiest Moment Was: _____

_____

_____

What Do You Want To Be When You Grow Up *More*? _____

_____

_____

DECEMBER 21, 20___

About Today: _____

_____

_____

_____

You're Grateful For: _____

Your Happiest Moment Was: _____

_____

_____

If You Could Live Anywhere In The World, Where Would You Live & Why?

_____

_____

DECEMBER 21, 20___

About Today: _____

_____

_____

_____

You're Grateful For: _____

Your Happiest Moment Was: _____

_____

_____

If You Could Live Anywhere In The World, Where Would You Live & Why?

_____

_____

DECEMBER 22, 20____

About Today: _____

_____

_____

_____

You're Grateful For: _____

Your Happiest Moment Was: _____

_____

_____

Do You Generally Contribute Positive Or Negative Energy To A Room?

_____

_____

DECEMBER 22, 20____

About Today: _____

_____

_____

_____

You're Grateful For: _____

Your Happiest Moment Was: _____

_____

_____

Do You Generally Contribute Positive Or Negative Energy To A Room?

_____

_____

DECEMBER 23, 20___

About Today: _____

_____

_____

_____

You're Grateful For: _____

Your Happiest Moment Was: _____

_____

_____

What Are You Avoiding? Why? _____

_____

_____

DECEMBER 23, 20___

About Today: _____

_____

_____

_____

You're Grateful For: _____

Your Happiest Moment Was: _____

_____

_____

What Are You Avoiding? Why? _____

_____

_____

DECEMBER 24, 20____

About Today: _____

_____

_____

_____

You're Grateful For: _____

Your Happiest Moment Was: _____

_____

_____

How Often Do You Compare Yourself To Those Less Fortunate? _____

_____

_____

DECEMBER 24, 20____

About Today: _____

_____

_____

_____

You're Grateful For: _____

Your Happiest Moment Was: _____

_____

_____

How Often Do You Compare Yourself To Those Less Fortunate? _____

_____

_____

DECEMBER 25, 20____

About Today: _____

_____

_____

_____

You're Grateful For: _____

Your Happiest Moment Was: _____

_____

_____

Do You Find Yourself Influencing Your World, Or It Influencing You?

_____

_____

DECEMBER 25, 20____

About Today: _____

_____

_____

_____

You're Grateful For: _____

Your Happiest Moment Was: _____

_____

_____

Do You Find Yourself Influencing Your World, Or It Influencing You?

_____

_____

DECEMBER 26, 20____

About Today: _____

_____

_____

_____

You're Grateful For: _____

Your Happiest Moment Was: _____

_____

_____

What Do You Allow To Distract You From Your Goals? _____

_____

_____

DECEMBER 26, 20____

About Today: _____

_____

_____

_____

You're Grateful For: _____

Your Happiest Moment Was: _____

_____

_____

What Do You Allow To Distract You From Your Goals? _____

_____

_____

DECEMBER 27, 20___

About Today: _____

_____

_____

_____

You're Grateful For: _____

Your Happiest Moment Was: _____

_____

_____

Rate Your Day On A Scale Of 1–10. If Not A 10, What Could Have Made It One?

_____

_____

DECEMBER 27, 20___

About Today: _____

_____

_____

_____

You're Grateful For: _____

Your Happiest Moment Was: _____

_____

_____

Rate Your Day On A Scale Of 1–10. If Not A 10, What Could Have Made It One?

_____

_____

DECEMBER 28, 20____

About Today: _____

_____

_____

_____

You're Grateful For: _____

Your Happiest Moment Was: _____

_____

_____

Are You Allowing Something/Someone To Hurt Or Abuse You? _____

_____

_____

DECEMBER 28, 20____

About Today: _____

_____

_____

_____

You're Grateful For: _____

Your Happiest Moment Was: _____

_____

_____

Are You Allowing Something/Someone To Hurt Or Abuse You? _____

_____

_____

DECEMBER 29, 20____

About Today: _____

_____

_____

_____

You're Grateful For: _____

Your Happiest Moment Was: _____

_____

_____

In What Ways Did You Grow This Year? _____

_____

_____

DECEMBER 29, 20____

About Today: _____

_____

_____

_____

You're Grateful For: _____

Your Happiest Moment Was: _____

_____

_____

In What Ways Did You Grow This Year? _____

_____

_____

DECEMBER 30, 20____

About Today: _____

_____

_____

_____

You're Grateful For: _____

Your Happiest Moment Was: _____

_____

_____

What Was Your Happiest Moment This Year? _____

_____

_____

DECEMBER 30, 20____

About Today: _____

_____

_____

_____

You're Grateful For: _____

Your Happiest Moment Was: _____

_____

_____

What Was Your Happiest Moment This Year? _____

_____

_____

DECEMBER 31, 20____

About Today: _____

_____

_____

_____

You're Grateful For: _____

Your Happiest Moment Was: _____

_____

_____

What Was Your Greatest Accomplishment This Year? _____

_____

_____

DECEMBER 31, 20____

About Today: _____

_____

_____

_____

You're Grateful For: _____

Your Happiest Moment Was: _____

_____

_____

What Was Your Greatest Accomplishment This Year? _____

_____

_____

A LOT CAN HAPPEN IN A YEAR

About Jessica A. Walsh

Jessica A. Walsh is a writer, wellness blogger and editor. Her quest to live a happier, gentler, and more compassionate life is chronicled at **www.jessicaannwalsh.com**. Please join in her journey towards personal, spiritual, and physical growth by subscribing to her newsletter.

Walsh is currently writing her first novel, a women's domestic drama inspired by her journey and experiences with addiction and mental illness. Her prior works can be found in *Chicken Soup for the Soul: My Very Good, Very Bad Dog* (2016) and *Reading Glasses: Stories Through An Unpredictable Lens* (Hypothetical Press, 2014), which she also co-edited. Walsh serves as Vice President of Programming for the South Jersey Writers' Group.

She also enjoys practicing yoga and meditation, reading and cooking. She attempts to live a simpler and more minimalist lifestyle in New Jersey with her husband and dog.

Please stay in touch!

Photo by Ali Brant Photography

Website: www.jessicaannwalsh.com
Twitter: Jessica_A_Walsh
Facebook: jessicaannwalsh
Instagram: jessica_a_walsh
Pinterest: Jessica_A_Walsh

A firm believer in the positive powers of journaling, she found lugging around multiple books both cumbersome and impractical. This journal was born out of her desire to have one place to capture all the components of her journaling practice: gratitude, happiness, and daily reflection, along with a supply of thought-provoking questions.

Reviews are critical to a book's exposure. If you enjoy *Questions for Life* please consider leaving a review on Amazon so that others may also experience this journal. Thank you!

Made in the USA
San Bernardino, CA
12 July 2017